ACCOUNTING EDUCATION IN SOUTH ASIA

About the Author

K.R. Sharma is currently Professor of Commerce, Mizoram University, Aizawl, and former Professor, Chairman Faculty of Commerce and Dean College of Commerce and Management Studies, M. L. Sukhadia University, Udaipur with over 43 years experience of teaching post-graduate courses in Management and Commerce. He was deputed by Ministry of External Affairs, Government of India as Professor of Business Administration at the Institute of Management, Tribhuwan University, Kathmandu-Nepal for two years (1986-1987) under Colombo Plan and was UGC Visiting Professor at M.D.S. University, Ajmer for one year (1999-2000).

Apart from completing two major research projects, UGC (1988-1992) and ICSSR (1994-98) a minor research project UGC (1980-1982), Dr. Sharma has supervised 15 works leading to Ph.D. degree.

Dr. Sharma was National President of Indian Accounting Association (1996-97), President, Rajasthan Vanijya Parishad (1999-2000), Chief Editor, *Indian Journal of Accounting* (1998-2001) and is Life Member of Indian Accounting Association, Udaipur, Accounting Research Foundation, Calcutta, All India Commerce Association, New Delhi, Indian Society for Training & Development, New Delhi, and Rajasthan Vanijya Parishad, Udaipur.

Dr. Sharma is author of *Operations Research and Quantitative Techniques* (Kalyani Publishers, Ludhiana), *Project Management* (National Publishing House, New Delhi) and *Research Methodology* (National Publishing House, New Delhi).

ACCOUNTING EDUCATION IN SOUTH ASIA

K.R. Sharma
Professor of Commerce,
Mizoram University
Aizawl, Mizoram

CONCEPT PUBLISHING COMPANY, NEW DELHI-110 059

The views and opinions expressed in this book are those of the author and do not necessarily reflect the views of the organization to which he belongs.

ISBN-81-8069-042-3

First Published 2004

Published and Printed by
Ashok Kumar Mittal
Concept Publishing Company
A/15-16, Commercial Block, Mohan Garden
NEW DELHI-110 059 (India)

Phones : 25351460, 25351794
Fax : 0091-11-25357103
E-mail : publishing@conceptpub.com

"Any satisfactory system of education should aim at a balanced growth of the individual and insist on both knowledge and wisdom. (Gyanam Vigyanam Sahitam). It should not only train the intellect but also bring grace into the heart of man. If we do not have a general philosophy or attitude of life, our minds will be confused, and we suffer from greed, pusillanimity, anxiety and defeatism. Mental slums are more dangerous to mankind than material slums."

– Sarvapalli Radhakrishnan

PREFACE

The global economic scene is changing. The socio-cultural environment in the countries of South Asia is also changing. This great continent, which has been the cradle of two most important civilizations, is also on the move. National boundaries are breaking and the business is becoming global. Accountants, as the conscience keepers of business and also as protectors of public interest, have an important role in this process of change.

The research project entitled *Accounting Education in South Asia* , sponsored by the Indian Council of Social Sciences Research, New Delhi, based on a comprehensive survey of the policies of the governments and their outcome and activities of the social and economic institutions at work in the field of education in general and accounting education in particular, was an effort to analyze and understand this change.

The subject of research has been close to my heart. As a senior faculty member in the Department of Accounting in one of the leading universities of India, as Colombo Plan Expert in Nepal, as President of Indian Accounting Association and as Chief Editor of *Indian Journal of Accounting,* I had many occasions to discuss, deliberate and write on the subject and present the findings at a number of forums and on a number of occasions. Some of the papers on the subject, presented at the seminars and published from time to time, are listed in the bibliography. The present work is the culmination of this abiding interest in the subject.

The policy makers in governments as well as in business enterprises recognize the lack of adequate and quality information as a major impediment in their work. An attempt has been made in the present work to put a broad range of information related with the subject at one place. The results may be of interest to planners, policy makers, educators and professionals at different levels in governments, universities and bodies of professional accountants.

It gives me great pleasure to place the report of the research work before the discerning readers for inquiry and debate. I take this opportunity to put on record my gratitude to the Indian Council of Social Sciences Research for financial support, and to a large number of friends and well-wishers from academy and profession, who provided information to make this happen.

K. R. Sharma

CONTENTS

LIST OF TABLES

LIST OF ABBREVIATIONS

ACA	- Association Member of Institute of Chartered Accountants
ADB	- Asian Development Bank
ADFIAP	- Association of Development Institutions in Asia and the Pacific
AECC	- Accounting Education Change Commission
AFTA	- ASEAN Free Trade Area
AICTE	- All India Council of Technical Education
AMDISA	- Association of Management Development Institutions in South Asia
ASEAN	- Association of South East Asian Nations
BIMSTEC	- Bangladesh, India, Myanmar, Sri Lanka and Thailand Economic Commission
CAPA	- Confederation of Asian and Pacific Accountants
CDC	- Curriculum Development Centre
DGFT	- Director General Foreign Trade
ET	- Economic Times
EU	- European Union
FCA	- Fellow Member of Institute of Chartered Accountants
HDI	- Human Development Index
IAA	- Indian Accounting Association
IAAER	- International Association for Accounting Education and Research
ICAI	- Institute of Chartered Accountants of India
ICAB	- Institute of Chartered Accountants of Bangladesh
ICAN	- Institute of Chartered Accountants of Nepal
ICAP	- Institute of Chartered Accountants of Pakistan
ICASI	- Institute of Chartered Accountants of Sri Lanka
CMAB	- Institute of Cost & Management Accountants of Bangladesh

ICMAP	-	Institute of Cost & Management Accountants of Pakistan
ICSSR	-	Indian Council of Social Sciences Research
ICWA	-	Institute of Cost and Works Accountants of India
IFAC	-	International Federation of Accountants
SAARC	-	South Asian Association for Regional Cooperation
SAFA	-	South Asian Federation of Accountants
SAFTA	-	South Asian Free Trade Area
SAPTA	-	South Asian Preferential Trade Agreement
SCCI	-	SAARC Chamber of Commerce and Industry
UGC	-	University Grants Commission

1

INTRODUCTION

Statement of the Problem

Education plays a vital role in the process of development, and also in the improvement of quality of life for individuals as well as the society as a whole. In this context it is worthwhile to note that article 26 of the Universal Declaration on Human Rights proclaimed by the General Assembly of the United Nations in 1948 stated that "everyone has the right of education". The World Conference on Education (1990) had recommended that "education for all by the year 2000 should be the target for the member states." Under the 'Programme of Education for All by the Year 2000' the target to operationalise it emphasized upon not only literacy and adult education but also upon raising the common level of learning achievement.

The South Asian region comprises of India, Pakistan, Bangladesh, Nepal, Bhutan, Maldives, Sri Lanka, Burma, Singapore and Afghanistan. Of these the first seven countries have formed an association for regional cooperation, known as South Asian Association for Regional Cooperation (SAARC), with its headquarter at Kathmandu, Nepal. All these countries are developing countries with poor infrastructure base, heavy pressure of population, low per capita income and high level of illiteracy and infant mortality.

Education is the single most important factor, which assists in improving skills, which, in turn, raise productivity and wealth. Income, in turn, is needed to finance educational programmes. The relationship between education and economic development, therefore, is reciprocal. (Ansari, 1987 p.6) Education is needed for strengthening the human factor, which interacts with all other factors of production at every stage and in varying capacities. This is applicable to accounting education also.

The accounting education systems in these countries, following their economic development effort, have not maintained the same levels as those in the developing countries. Of these India alone can be recognized as an advanced country, so far as accounting education is concerned. However, in general a lack of accounting academics, professionals and accounting education infrastructure is notable in the countries of this region.

Flow of funds from international financial institutions, intercountry economic assistance and investment by private sector are essential for the economic development of these countries. But besides eligible and competent individuals and institutions, the capability of ensuring proper accountability, a well-established accounting system and audit by independent authority are necessary conditions for such an investment. Similarly for ensuring efficiency and productivity support systems, such as managerial accounting, budgetary control, cost control, etc. are needed. Thus considering the economic situation in the region there is a pressing need for establishing a system of accounting based on such essential features as transparency, understandability, accountability in government, in public orgnisations, in business etc. This can be brought about only through accounting education.

Development of accounting education shall require objective comprehension of current status and problems of accounting education in the countries of this region. One such survey was carried out by the author during his association with the Institute of Management, Tribhuwan University, Kathmandu, Nepal, as a Colombo Plan Professor of Business Administration. The results of the study were presented at the IVth International Conference on Accounting Education and Research at Kyoto, Japan, held from October 7 to 10, 1987. This covered the status and the problems of accounting education in Nepal. The report was later on published in the *Indian Journal of Accounting,* Volume XXVII, December 1987. The present work is a follow-up of the above report covering all the seven countries, which are members of SAARC.

Review of Literature

Scanning through the libraries it was observed that the existing literature on the subject was scanty. Though 'accounting education' has been a topic of discussion and debate at the seminars organized during the annual conferences of the Indian Accounting Association, papers have been presented by the scholars. This has formed an important topic in the presidential speech of the president of Indian Accounting Association. Yet no study has been done so far on the subject with a wider geographical focus. Among the important works, which have made significant contribution to existing literature, on education in general and accounting education in particular, in the region may be included the reports of various committees and commissions set up by Governments in India, *History of the Accounting Profession in India* Vol. I (Kapadia, 1972), 'A Survey of Research in Accounting Theory' (Bhandari, 1976), 'Commerce Education in India, (Bhorali, 1987), 'Present Status and Problems of Accounting Education in Nepal' (Sharma, 1987), 'Current Status and Development of Accounting Education in CAPA' (Hiroshi Kawakita, 1987), 'Recent Trends in Commerce and Management Education' (Khanzode, 1990), 'Report of the UGC Curriculum Development Center in Commerce' (UGC, 1989), 'Statements of Accounting Education Change Commission' (AECC, 1990-93) and 'Accounting Education in India' (Banerjee, 1994).

Since independence the Government of India has appointed a number of committees and commissions to study the crisis in education in general and higher education in particular. The reports of these bodies have formed the basis of policies formulated and thus provided direction to the growth of education in India. Among these the University Education Commission 1948-49 (Radhakrishnan Commission) examined the development of higher education and made proposals for its future expansion and improvement. A similar inquiry with regard to secondary education was carried out by the Secondary

Education Commission 1952-53 (Mudaliar Commission). Both the commissions, however, looked at education in compartmentalized fashion, as higher education and secondary education, while it is not so, and ignored primary education, adult education etc.

The Education Commission 1964-65 (Kothari Commission) may be regarded as the first commission in India to look comprehensively at almost all aspects of education and evolve a blueprint for national system of education. The National Policy on Education, 1968 was designed based on the recommendations of the Commission. The National Policy on Education, 1979 was also influenced by the report of the Commission.

The National Education Policy, 1986 was yet another landmark in the direction of making the education system relevant to the need of the changing times. It adopted a positive approach and declared education a unique investment in the present and the future. It was resolved that all children who attained the age of about 11 years by 1990 will have had at least 5 years or its equivalent of schooling, and further that, by 1995 all children will be provided free and compulsory education up to the age of 14. It also declared that by 1990 and 1995, vocational courses would respectively cover about 10 to 15 per cent of the higher secondary students. It reaffirmed that education will be treated as a crucial area of investment for national development and survival, and that it will be ensured that from the Eighth Five Year Plan onwards the investment in education will exceed 6 per cent of national income.

Shri G.P. Kapadia, the first President of the Institute of Chartered Accountants of India, has in the *History of Accounting Profession in India* after giving early history of commerce education in India, dealt with the growth of accounting profession in India, and the role of the Institute of Chartered Accountants of India in promoting professional accounting education. Some of the contemporary problems of the profession at that time, such as autonomy, reciprocity, professional ethics, professional development, arrangement for education and training of professional accountants, accounting research, splitting of the profession etc. have been also discussed. However, the focus of the work is limited to professional education and training and it does not cover the various aspects of accounting and commerce education in the universities.

Dr. Bhorali's book *Commerce Education in India,* is an edited volume, containing nineteen papers contributed by the authors at a seminar on the subject, organised by the Department of Commerce, Gauhati University, Guwahati. The authors have dealt with different aspects of commerce education and the problems faced, particularly in the northern region, in the papers. Thus the work provided a limited focus.

Based on the results of a survey undertaken in 1986-87 during deputation as Colombo Plan Professor of Business Administration at Tribhuwan University, Kathmandu (Nepal), a paper on 'Present Status and Problems of Accounting Education in Nepal' was presented by Dr. K.R. Sharma at the IV International Conference on Accounting Education at Kyoto (Japan) in October 1987, which was later on published in the *Indian Journal of Accounting,* Vol. XXVII, December 1987. The paper gives an assessment of the present position of accounting education in Tribhuwan University, Kathmandu, which was the only university imparting commerce and management education in Nepal at that time, and professional education of accounting in Nepal. Some problem areas have been highlighted and suggestions have been given for their solution. Yet the focus and the scope of the study was limited to a single country, Nepal.

Hiroshi Kawakita, the then president of Confederation of Asian and Pacific Accountants (CAPA), in a paper presented at the IV International Conference on Accounting Education at Kyoto (Japan) in October 1987 on 'Current Status and Development of Accounting Education in CAPA' (mimeographed) has, after summarizing the results of the survey of teaching resources for the development of accounting education in CAPA member organizations, identified important issues and challenges before these bodies. Though many of the issues and problems are common to all developing countries, yet due to cultural, social and economic differences these are not applicable as such to the South Asian countries.

Dr. V. V. Khanzode's book on *Recent Trends in Commerce and Management Education,* is a compendium of articles dealing with different aspects of business and business education. The book is divided into two sections, section I containing 14 articles covering the topics in theory and practice of business and management, and section II containing 18 articles on different aspects of commerce and management education. The book was basically developed as a course material for M.Phil and MBA students. Many important aspects of accounting education, therefore, are not even touched in the work.

The Curriculum Development Centre's Programme was taken up by the University Grants Commission in India to promote excellence in teaching. Though all the universities through their academic bodies continuously undertake this exercise, this one was to be an exercise at national level. The UGC Curriculum Development Centre in Commerce (Department of Commerce & Business Administration, University of Allahabad, Allahabad) undertook the task of restructuring and reframing the various university level courses in commerce.

The Centre in their report of 1989 have suggested various courses with two-fold objectives, viz., to covered latest advancement in the subject and emphasized more upon job oriented courses. The Report suggested new courses for undergraduate classes, B.Com. (Honors) – 18 papers in three years, B.Com. (Professional) – choice of 18 out of 30 papers in three years (specialization in any of the three fields), the specialized post-graduate courses, M.Com. (Accounting) – 11 papers, M.Com. (Business Studies) – 11 papers, and M.Com. (Business Economics)-11 papers, and eight one year post-graduate diploma courses. The report of the Centre forms an important landmark in the field of curriculum development at national level. However, the follow-up was ineffective, and many universities in the country did not adopt these courses.

The American Accounting Association had appointed the Accounting Education Change Commission in 1989. It was sponsored by the Sponsors' Education Task Force representing the largest public accounting firms in the United States of America. Its objective was to become a catalyst for improving the academic preparation of accountants so that the entrants to the accounting profession may possess skills, knowledge and attitude required for success in accounting career path. The members of the Commission were drawn from the universities, professional accounting firms and business.

The Commission had after deliberations published a set of seven small booklets/pamphlets, two position statements, viz., 'Objectives of Education for Accountants' in September 1990 and 'The First Course in Accounting' in June 1992, and five issue statements, viz., 'AECC Urges Priority for Teaching in Higher Education' in August 1990, 'AECC Urges Disciplining of Academic Studies and Professional Accounting Examination Preparation' in July 1991, 'The Importance of Two-Tier Colleges for Accounting Education' in August 1992, 'Improving the Early Employment Experience of Accountants' in April 1993 and 'Evaluating and Rewarding Effective Teaching' in April 1993.

The Commission on the realization that accounting programmes have not kept pace with the dynamic, complex, expanding and constantly changing profession, for which students are being educated, set out its views on various issues to provide a focus for those participating in the task of imparting accounting education. The views presented are very useful for the development of accounting profession on sound lines. However, they had the conditions available in the United States of America in view. These, to an extent, are not applicable to developing countries.

Dr. Bhabtosh Banerjee in his book *Accounting Education in India* has dealt with the present status and different aspects of accounting education in India. The work is based on information collected from 39 universities, 2 professional institutes, 139 participants at various orientation and refresher courses organised by the academic staff colleges in different universities, and some professional accountants through a questionnaire formulated for the purpose. The problems faced at different levels have been identified and suggestions have been given towards their solution. However, the coverage of the work is limited to accounting education provided by the university system in India only.

The present study thus is the first effort in the direction of dealing with all relevant aspects of accounting education comprehensively, covering seven important countries of South Asia, which are members of SAARC.

South Asian Association for Regional Cooperation (SAARC)

The countries of South Asia have formed an association for regional cooperation, known as South Asian Association for Regional Cooperation (SAARC). Bangladesh, Bhutan, India, Maldives, Nepal, Pakistan and Sri Lanka are its members.

The first formal initiative for regional cooperation in South Asia was taken by Late Ziaur Rehman, the then President of Bangladesh, on 2nd May 1980, when he instructed his Foreign Minister, Samsul Haque to take up the matter with the governments of other six countries of the region. A formal letter in this respect was sent to heads of governments of India, Pakistan, Sri Lanka, Bhutan, Nepal and Maldives on 25th November 1980. The matter was then discussed at Colombo, the capital of Sri Lanka, at the meeting of foreign ministers of these countries, from 21st to 23rd April 1981. Finally at the summit meeting attended by the heads of governments of these seven countries at Dhaka, the capital of Bangladesh, on 7th and 8th December 1985 the Charter of South Asian Association for Regional Cooperation was approved and the Association was given a formal shape.

The objectives and principles of SAARC are as under :

Objectives

- To promote the welfare of the peoples of South Asia and to improve their quality of life;
- To accelerate economic growth, social progress and cultural development in the region and to provide all individuals the opportunity to live in dignity and to realise their full potential;
- To promote and strengthen collective self-reliance among the countries of South Asia;
- To contribute to mutual trust, understanding and appreciation of one another's problems;
- To promote collaboration and mutual assistance in the economic, social, cultural and scientific fields;
- To strengthen cooperation with other developing countries;

- To strengthen cooperation among themselves in international forums on matters of common interest; and
- To cooperate with international and regional organisations with similar aims and purposes.

Principles

- Cooperation within the framework of the Association is based on the respect for the principles of sovereign equality, territorial integrity, political independence, and non-interference in the internal affairs of other states and mutual benefits.
- Such cooperation is to implement and not to substitute bilateral or multilateral cooperation.
- Such cooperation should be consistent with bilateral and multilateral obligations of the member states.

Thus SAARC is a manifestation of the determination of people of South Asia to involve cooperation in solving problems specific to the region, strengthen collective self-reliance and accelerate economic, social and cultural development of the countries of the region.

The secretariat of South Asian Association for Regional Cooperation is at Kathmandu, Nepal. The present Secretary General of the Association is Naeem U Hasan.

All important decisions regarding the activities of the SAARC are taken at summit meetings attended by heads of governments of member countries. The first summit meeting was held in Dhaka in 1985, the second in Bangalore in 1986, the third in Kathmandu in 1987, the fourth in Islamabad in 1988, the fifth in Male in November 1990, the sixth in Colombo in 1991, the seventh in Dhaka in April 1993, eighth in 1995, the ninth at Male in May 1997 and the tenth in Colombo in July 1998. The eighth summit meeting was proposed to be held at Kathmandu, Nepal in November 1999. However, the Kargil conflict between India and Pakistan and military takeover and change of government in Pakistan created conditions whereby it had to be deferred. The next meeting of SAARC is proposed to be held at

Islamabad, Pakistan in January 2003. Thus over the past fifteen years SAARC could hold only ten summit meetings.

Important issues discussed at these meetings included, curbing terrorist activity, the Maldivian initiative for international consensus on reinforcing the security of small countries, effective steps to combat narco-terrorism, collective stand on regional and local environmental issues, establishment of a regional development fund, establishment of a South Asian Commission on Poverty Alleviation, Human Rights and Democracy in the Third World Countries, Child Survival, Protection and Development, Achievement of Total Primary Education for Children by the year 2000 by sharing technical know-how and expertise, preferential trade arrangement, free trade area etc.

Regional cooperation under SAARC was initially limited to 5 areas of technical cooperation. The scope of regional cooperation has been gradually increased to 12 areas and it now constitutes an Integrated Programme of Action. The areas of cooperation are agriculture, environment, communication, rural development, science and technology and prevention of drug trafficking abuse.

The year 1990 was observed as 'the SAARC Year of Girl Child', 1991 as 'the SAARC Year of Shelter', 1992 as 'the SAARC Year of Environment', 1993 as 'the SAARC Year of Disabled Persons' etc.

Important institutions set up by SAARC are, the Human Resource Development Center at Islamabad, the Regional Tuberculosis Center at Kathmandu, the Regional Documentation Center at New Delhi and the Agricultural Information Center at New Delhi.

Thus, SAARC is emerging as a useful forum for promoting understanding and greater regional cooperation for social, cultural and economic development of the people of this region, including education.

While SAARC has a wider focus, two regional bodies of professional accountants have been also set up and are actively functioning in the region, viz., the South Asian Federation of Accountants (SAFA) and the Confederation of Asian and Pacific Accountants (CAPA).

The South Asian Federation of Accountants (SAFA)

The South Asian Federation of Accountants (SAFA) a federation of accountants from South Asian countries was set up in 1984 at the initiative of India. Shri P. N. Shah, FCA, former president of the Institute of Chartered Accountants of India was elected as its first president. Eight bodies of the accountants from five member countries of SAARC are members of SAFA. These are :

Bangladesh	1. The Institute of Chartered Accountants of Bangladesh
	2. The Institute of Cost & Management Accountants of Bangladesh
India	1. The Institute of Chartered Accountants of India
	2. The Institute of Cost & Works Accountants of India
Nepal	1. The Institute of Chartered Accountants of Nepal
Pakistan	1. The Institute of Chartered Accountants of Pakistan
	2. The Institute of Cost & Management Accountants of Pakistan
Sri Lanka	1. The Institute of Chartered Accountants of Sri Lanka.

The permanent secretariat of SAFA is located at the headquarter of the Institute of Chartered Accountants of India, Indraprastha Marg, New Delhi. Shri Ashok Haldia, Secretary of the Institute of Chartered Accountants of India is also secretary of SAFA.

Coordinated development of accounting education, harmonization of accounting practices, and professional development of accountants in the member countries are foremost among the objectives of SAFA.

The presidentship of SAFA is rotated among the member countries. Shri T.S. Vishwanath of the Institute of Chartered Accountants of India was president and Shri Lal Nanayakkara of the Institute of Chartered Accountants of Sri Lanka was vice president of SAFA for 1999.

The following have been the past Presidents of SAFA (SAFA Handbook, 1999):

1.	Shri P. N. Shah, FCA The Institute of Chartered Accountants of India	1985
2.	Shri L. R. Watawala The Institute of Chartered Accountants of Sri Lanka	1986
3.	Shri E. S. H. Dahodwala The Institute of Chartered Accountants of Pakistan	1987
4.	Shri M. Yunus The Institute of Chartered Accountants of Bangladesh	1988
5.	Shri V. Kalyanaraman The Institute of Cost & Works Accountants of India	1989
6.	Mian Mumtaz Abdullah The Institute of Cost & Management Accountants of Pakistan	1990
7.	Shri Habibur Rahman The Institute of Cost & Management Accountants of Bangladesh	1991
8.	Shri K. M. Agrawal The Institute of Chartered Accountants of India	1992
9.	Shri N. A. L. Cabraal The Institute of Chartered Accountants of Sri Lanka	1993
10.	Shri Ebrahim Sidat The Institute of Chartered Accountants of Pakistan	1994
11.	Shri Jamal Uddin Ahmad The Institute of Chartered Accountants of Bangladesh	1995
12.	Shri K. R. S. Sastry The Institute of Cost & Works Accountants of India	1996
13.	Shri Khawaja Amjad Saeed The Institute of Cost & Management Accountants of Pakistan	1997
14.	Ch. Hafizur Rahman The Institute of Cost & Management Accountants of Bangladesh	1998

The Confederation of Asian and Pacific Accountants (CAPA)

The Confederation of Asian and Pacific Accountants (CAPA) is a federation of regional organizations of the International Federation of Accountants (IFAC). 29 bodies of accountants from 21 countries of Asia and Pacific region are members of CAPA. The member countries of CAPA may broadly be placed into three categories, viz. developed countries, such as Australia, Canada, Japan, New Zealand and the USA, newly industrialized countries, such as Hong Kong, South Korea, Singapore, Taiwan, Thailand, Malaysia, Indonesia, Cambodia, and developing countries, such as India, the Philippines, Pakistan, Bangladesh and Sri Lanka. The countries in the region, which are not members of CAPA, include Burma, Vietnam, Laos, the Peoples Republic of China and North Korea. (Kawakita, 1987)

The Institute of Chartered Accountants of India and the Institute of Cost & Works Accountants of India are member bodies of CAPA from India. The Institute of Chartered Accountants of India and the Institute of Cost & Works Accountants of India had jointly hosted the X CAPA conference at New Delhi from 21st to 25th November 1983. The theme of the Conference was "Accounting and Society".

It is observed that among the member countries the developed countries are advanced in economic terms and the same can be said about their accounting education systems. Among these Japan has continuously followed the continental statute law (German and French laws) system, while other countries follow the Anglo American legal system. The economic growth in the newly industrialized Asian countries has been remarkable and happily their accounting education systems have also maintained level with the economic growth. Among the developing countries it is significant to note that India and the Philippines may be recognized as advanced countries, so far as accounting education is concerned. However, there is in general a lack of sound accounting education system and accounting professionals in these countries. (Kawakita, 1987)

Since its establishment the Confederation has shown strong interest in the development of accounting education in the countries of Asia and Pacific region. The International

Federation of Accountants (IFAC), the Asian Development Bank (ADB) and the World Bank (WB) had promoted an 'Asia and Pacific Conference on Accounting Education for Development' in November 1984 in Manila. Out of 193 participants from 38 countries at the Conference 111 participants were from 27 Asian countries. A 'Regional Symposium on Financial Control, Accounting and Auditing Practices of Development Financing Institutions', jointly sponsored by the Association of Development Financing Institutions in Asia and the Pacific (ADFIAP) and the Asian Development Bank (ADB) was held at Manila in 1987.

Conceptual Framework

Accounting supplies much of the comprehensive and dependable information that management needs to control and administer resources in its charge efficiently and productively. It also supplies data that management needs to fulfil its responsibility to report to owners, creditors, government and others with bona fide interests. In turn these owners, creditors, governments and others rely on accounting reports to assist them in determining and evaluating the performance of the management and the business systems. Accounting thus is essential to effective functioning of any organization, particularly the business organizations with corporate status.

Public accountability is an essential condition for fair and efficient investment and therefore, there must be eligible and competent individuals and institutions that may ensure proper accountability. It may be pertinent here to quote from the status report. It mentions that:

"1. *The Assurance of Economic Fairness with regard to Investment :* Although active investments are being made, such investments can be undermined when the investors maintain their accounts in a perfunctory manner or make false statements in the accounts. Well-established accounting systems and audit systems and their appropriate operation in countries in which investment has been made must be a necessary condition for investment. Also, it goes without saying that capable accounting technicians, who are capable, and a continuous accounting education system, which is adequate for operating the above systems are indispensable."

"2. *Assurance of Investment Efficiency* : When investments are used ineffectively, such that economic results are poor, the investments lose their original objectives. In order to secure such desired investment efficiency, invests should maintain their accounting practices at the highest levels of quality possible and improve the productivity of their investments. In order to ensure that productivity is maintained, managerial accounting, especially budget control and cost management for target management is required. Training of eligible human resources is also necessary."(Kawakita 1987, pp.2-3)

In case of developing countries active investment from private sector and financial assistance from international financial institutions, such as the World Bank (WB), the Asian Development Bank (ADB), the Overseas Economic Cooperation Fund (OECF) etc., is necessary. However, the assurance of economic fairness with regard to investment, and assurance of economic efficiency, are the two necessary conditions for such financial assistance also.

It needs no emphasis to understand that accounting education provides the foundation not only for the adoption of sound accounting systems and practices but also for economic development.

Accounting courses are taught as a part of Commerce and Management disciplines in all educational institutions including universities of the region. The emphasis of course differs from country to country and also from one university to another, within the same country. However, courses such as 'financial accounting', 'cost accounting', 'corporate accounting', 'government accounting', 'multi-national accounting', 'international accounting' etc., are taught at degree and post-graduate levels in all these countries. Some universities also conduct teaching of specialized degree and diploma courses in Accounting, such as 'Diploma in Cost & Management Accounting', 'Diploma in Internal Auditing', 'Diploma in Taxation', 'Diploma in

Management Accounting', 'Diploma in Corporate Accounting', 'Master of Finance and Control', etc.

The bodies of professional accountants have an important role in the education and training of professional accountants. Nature and coverage of their education programme, the curriculum and the provision for on the job training and exposure of the students to the world of work, make these programmes different from the generalized accounting education courses of the universities. However, there are differences in the education programmes of the bodies of professional accountants from country to country.

This project had focused on accounting education in wider sense, which covered both the streams, the education provided by the university system as well as the education provided by the bodies of professional accountants. Accordingly the areas such as the coverage, the breadth and the depth of knowledge, proficiency expected, exposure to real life situations during training, understanding and proficiency in the use of information technology in accounting etc. have been probed in the light of changing structure of the society, the education system, the economies and the business organizations in different countries of the region.

Scope

The scope of the present study is limited to seven countries of South Asia, which have formed an association for regional cooperation, known as SAARC. These countries are Bangladesh, Bhutan, India, Maldives, Nepal, Pakistan and Sri Lanka. In spite of significant differences in size, resource endowment, stage of development, these countries have a common cultural heritage and strong religious and cultural affinity. While each country has its national language and also some regional languages, English has been retained as a common link language. It is now being widely accepted as the language of business world.

Half a century back some of these countries formed part of the British Empire and as such have inherited the British administrative and education systems. These countries have tried to carve out an identity of their own during the last fifty years and have initiated the process of development as per their need and resources. There is a strong urge in these countries to develop themselves as powerful national entities. These countries maintain diplomatic, cultural and economic relations with each other. The smaller countries have tried to emulate the larger countries, and have forged new economic ties based on mutual benefit. In fact, SAARC is the natural outcome of such an urge.

Burma and Afghanistan have not been included in the study due to their slightly distinct identities, their past as well as the present. Both these countries have maintained outside contacts at minimum level. Burma has followed isolationist policy during the last 30 years and has almost sealed its borders with neighbouring countries. Afghanistan was under political and military influence of Soviet Russia for a long period of time, and following the civil war it remained under the control of Taliban, a group of Islamic fundamentalist militants inspired and supported by Pakistan. It is a war torn country, where the course of events has always remained uncertain and even now the future of this country of simple and brave Pathans is uncertain. Considering its history, culture and economic relations it can be more suitably placed with Central Asian countries. The language of these countries also formed a significant barrier in external communication.

Singapore, another small country, rather a small island, with a social and economic set up which is far different from that of other countries of the region, can also be not placed with the South Asian countries. Devoid of a natural resource base, it has carved a nitche of its own, as an international trading and financial centre. Singapore has preferred to become a member of the Association of East Asian Nations (ASIAN).

Accounting education in the countries of the region has certain common features. Major countries of the region, India, Pakistan, Bangladesh and Sri Lanka were under British influence for about 200 years. Undivided India, consisting of present India, Pakistan and Bangladesh, remained under direct British rule for 100 years, while Sri Lanka remained under British rule from 1815 to 1948. Nepal, Bhutan and Maldives were small countries, though strategically significant for the British government, and as such the British rulers maintained intimate relationship with the rulers in these countries. The education systems of all these countries thus were patterned on the British system. Some changes of course have been made in the education systems during the last fifty years following their independence from the British rule. Each country has tried to evolve its own education system. However, the significant common features still remain. This greatly facilitated a comparative study.

Thus, apart from being neighbour, these countries have a common heritage and strong geographic, economic and cultural affinity. English is being retained as a common link language by these countries. Their education systems are based on the British system, and so also their civil administration. There are no significant travel restrictions. The information could, therefore, be collected with some effort.

The Accounting education systems have not remained unaffected by the politico-economic changes in these countries. To begin with accounting education was regarded as mainly vocational. Even now unlike the United States of America, Japan, Australia, the United Kingdom, Accounting is not recognized as a separate discipline at under-graduate and post-graduate levels by most of the universities in the countries of the region. Accounting forms part of commerce and business management courses. Emphasis of course differs from country to country and also from region to region in the same country.

The bodies of professional accountants have been set up in India, Pakistan, Bangladesh, Sri Lanka and Nepal through statutes. Apart from regulation and control of the profession, these Institutes have made significant contribution for the cause of accounting education in the region. The responsibility of accounting education in the region thus is shared by a number of different organizations. The prominent among these are the following:

(i) Institutes of Professional Accountants
(ii) Institutes of Business Management
(iii) Universities and Colleges

(iv) Boards of Secondary Education and Secondary and Senior Secondary Schools
(v) Multinational Educational Institutes
(vi) Private Educational Institutions functioning as affiliated or accredited institutions or as registered bodies.

However, for the purpose of the present work all these bodies have been classified into two broad groups, the university system and the professional education system.

Research Objectives

Main objectives of the present study were:

1. To survey the laws, the statutes, the regulations, the accounting standards, the audit guidelines and the accounting practices in the countries of the region.
2. To examine the socio-economic profile and the emerging arrangement for economic cooperation, investment and trade promotion amongst SAARC countries.
3. To review the education system, the institutions and infrastructure for education and training of the academic accountants, and the arrangement for their continuing education in different countries of the region.
4. To examine the distinctive features and functioning of the arrangement for the education of the professional accountants and accounting technicians in different countries of the region.
5. To suggest a common approach for the development of a suitable accounting education system for the countries of the region.
6. To promote mutual understanding and respect for accounting, auditing and accounting education systems of different countries, and thereby contribute to regional cooperation.
7. To identify areas with potential for further research.

Hypotheses

The hypotheses taken for the study were :

1. The economic growth, investment and trade among the countries of the region have been significantly influenced by the growth of education in the countries of South Asian region.
2. The differences in statutes, regulatory framework, accounting standards, scope and status of accounting are not significant in the countries of the region.
3. The accounting education systems have been significantly influenced by social, economic and cultural differences in the countries of the region.
4. The bodies of professional accountants have made a significant contribution in the growth of professional education of accounting in the region.
5. Accounting education has made significant contribution to economic development of the countries of the region.
6. In spite of adverse socio-economic indicators there exists a strong base and potential for the growth of accounting education and development of accounting profession in the countries of the region.

Methodology of Research

The study has been based on secondary sources as well as an empirical investigation. To begin with the information available in the form of books, reports and articles available in the libraries of different institutions, which included the College of Commerce & Management Studies, Udaipur, Central Library, Mohan Lal Sukhadia University, Udaipur, Ratan Tata Memorial Library of Delhi University, Delhi, library of the Institute of Chartered Accountants of India, New Delhi, library of the Institute of Cost & Works Accountants of India, Calcutta and the library of the SAARC Secretariat at Kathmandu were scanned. A review of some of the works consulted is given in the survey of literature.

A comprehensive list of the universities, the management institutes and other educational institutions active in the region in the field of business education was prepared, based on the information given in the Handbook of the Association of Commonwealth Universities, the Handbook of the Association of Indian Universities, the University Grants Commission, New Delhi and the All India Council of Technical Education. A list of the bodies of professional accountants in the region was also prepared, based on the information available from the Institute of Chartered Accountants of India, New Delhi. Both these lists formed the universe of institutions to be covered for collecting information during the survey.

Thereafter a pilot study was conducted. For this a questionnaire was designed, institutions to be contacted were identified, and a copy of the questionnaire was mailed through post to the heads of these institutions in India and abroad. It was satisfying to find that some institutions did respond positively and returned the filled questionnaires.

Based on the experience gained from the pilot survey, two separate questionnaires were designed, one for the university departments of commerce and of management and the other one for the institutions of professional accountants. The two questionnaires are given as *Appendix 1.A* and *Appendix 1.B* respectively. Copies of these questionnaires were mailed to the heads of the departments of commerce and of management in case of university departments, and to the secretary of the institute, in the cases of institutions of professional accountants.

Since the questionnaires were mailed through post initially the response was not encouraging. A request letter was, therefore, again mailed as a reminder along with a copy of the questionnaire to the heads/secretaries. The request letter addressed to all these persons is given as *Appendix 1.C.* Efforts were also made through personal visits and mailing requests to friends and well-wishers for help in collecting the desired information. This brought positive results and better response. The names of the respondents are given in *Appendix 1.D.*

At a later stage since no visits could be undertaken to any of the countries outside India, some information was collected from the offices of the high commissioners and the embassies of the SAARC countries in New Delhi. The names and addresses of these offices are given in *Appendix 1.E.*

The present work thus is based on the information gathered from the secondary sources and also through an empirical investigation based on the questionnaires mailed through post to different category of respondents, and providing such information.

Descriptive approach has been adopted while drafting the report, in consideration of the nature of the subject matter of research project. Simple tables have been designed to give quantitative information pertaining to various aspects discussed in the text.

Chapter Scheme

The report has been organised in six chapters. In the first chapter are given the introduction of the problem, review of literature, areas of study, objectives, hypotheses, methodology of research, chapter scheme, limitations etc.

The second chapter describes the socio-economic profile and the emerging arrangement for economic cooperation, investment and trade promotion among the SAARC countries.

The status and the problems of education in general in the countries of the region have been discussed in the third chapter. The implications of the above and the long-term prospects have been also discussed here.

Besides country-wise position the over-all status of accounting education in the SAARC countries has been described in the fourth chapter. This covers the general business education provided under the university system and the management education.

The arrangement for the education and training of the professional accountants in the SAARC countries has been described in the fifth chapter. The emerging trends and the implications have been also analyzed in this chapter.

A summary of the conclusions and the problems of accounting education have been discussed in the sixth chapter. Based on this certain guidelines and suggestions for the development of accounting education in universities and colleges – departments of commerce/management and institutes of professional accountants have been given in this chapter.

Limitations

The research project was a regional study covering seven different countries of South Asia. This is a very difficult region for undertaking any research work. Though these countries have a common heritage and a long history of social, economic and diplomatic contacts, and to an extent their economies are inter-dependent, yet they are separate national entities. The association for regional cooperation, SAARC, is still in early stage of growth. The clouds of distrust and ego have not melted down and the achievements of SAARC cannot be considered as significant so far. However, this has been and remains a very useful forum, and may become in course of time a basis for economic union of the countries in the region.

The subject taken up for inquiry was new. No studies have been done so far covering this or a similar subject in India or any other country. Existing literature on the subject was found to be scanty and deficient in so many respects.

Accounting education is imparted by a variety of institutions at different levels. It forms part of the courses of study at the secondary and the senior secondary education, and as such looked after by the Boards of Secondary Education. At higher level the universities within their academic and territorial jurisdiction look after it. The professional education of accounting is the responsibility of national bodies of professional accountants. The governments as per their specific requirements and within their resources have made arrangement for education and training of government accountants. Some large employers like commercial banks, insurance companies, railways, post offices etc. have their own arrangement for training through specialized training centres. Coordinating with all these agencies proved to be very difficult task.

There is no regional body of academic institutions imparting accounting education. There is no common platform and forum for interaction on the subject. The regional body of the professional accountants, the South Asian Federation of Accountants (SAFA) is still in early stage of growth. Thus an institutional framework, which can provide basic infrastructure support for such a study did not exist. It was a great struggle to search for information and get it.

Travel to selected centres and institutions in all the countries of the region was a necessary requirement for the collection of information and developing first hand understanding of the problem. It was planned also. But due to a variety of reasons it could not be undertaken. The entire information, therefore, had to be collected by mailing the questionnaires through post and through personal contacts.

Obtaining information from different sources, the university departments of commerce and management and the institutions of professional accountants, proved to be a difficult exercise. This required repeated communications through post and use of personal contacts. Yet complete information could not be obtained. Wherever the information was found to be deficient it had to be supplemented from the secondary sources. All these efforts had their obvious limitations.

Still it may be asserted with confidence that breaking a new ground the present study is expected to provide a sound basis for undertaking regional studies on similar and related subjects. This is also expected to prove a very useful basis for initiating programmes for the development of accounting education in the SAARC countries and inter-country cooperation in this field.

2

SOCIO-ECONOMIC PROFILE

Introduction

Asia is a huge continent. It surpasses all other continents in area, population, size and resource base. It has rich and varied cultural heritage. It is home of world's two oldest civilizations, viz., the Chinese and the Indian. Asia at the same time is a continent of diversity in culture, history, language, ethnicity, religion, traditions and also in stage of growth and systems of economic and social development. Beyond culture and history, the vitality of Asian people has found expression in industrial growth and trade expansion and some of its dynamic economies are highly competitive and impact world markets. This has created a notion that economic dynamism will gradually shift from North Atlantic to Asian rim of the Pacific and the Indian Ocean in the next century.

Asia can be divided into three distinct regions, viz., East Asia, Southeast Asia and South Asia, with each region containing an assortment of countries following fairly similar development strategies. China, Japan, North Korea, South Korea, Taiwan and Hongkong form part of East Asia. Southeast Asia comprises of Laos, Kampuchea, Vietnam, Brunei, Indonesia, Malaysia, the Philippines, Singapore and Thailand. These countries had formed an association known as the Association of Southeast Asian Nations (ASEAN) on 8th August 1967. These countries have increasingly turned outward looking. South Asia, also known as the Indian Subcontinent, comprises of India, Pakistan, Sri Lanka, Bangladesh, Nepal,

Bhutan, Maldives, Burma and Afghanistan. Among these the first seven countries are members of SAARC.

Except for the socialist and the semi-socialist countries and the countries of South Asia with colonial background, international economic forces have played a pivotal role in the growth of these countries, particularly the export oriented ASEAN countries. Their exports have been mainly destined for the markets of industrialized countries of Europe, America and Japan. The exports consist of primary products and some manufactured products. In return they import capital goods and consumer durables. Some of these countries like Taiwan, South Korea, the Philippines and Indonesia have become excessively dependent upon industrialized countries, even when the economies of South Asian countries have remained more inward looking. However, these countries have established useful trade relations with neighbouring countries.

The economically well developed East Asian countries have achieved a relatively higher level of social development in terms of education, health care and desirable demographic trends while the countries of South Asia have accomplished lower social development besides lower level of income and its inequitable distribution. The countries of Southeast Asia may be placed somewhere between the two groups of countries, in terms of economic growth as well as social development.

Apart from trade the Asian countries are faced with the enormous challenge of mobilizing sufficient financial resources out of their savings to meet foreign exchange requirement for development and also to meet the trade shortfalls. Such additional resources can come only from external flows, usually from capital surplus countries. The private financial flows mainly take the form of either foreign direct investment or foreign commercial lending including short-term credit from banks and export credit agencies. While the East Asian and ASEAN countries have been able to attract adequate financial flows because of their open economies, the same is not the case with South Asian countries. Gradually after 1990 the developing countries have taken larger exposure in these countries. However, economic integration of Asia with the rest of the world greatly depends upon multi-national as well as regional flow of funds.

South Asia

South Asia is a region of garland countries. Garland symbolizes its unity in diversity. It is evocative of common culture and ethos that bind them together as people from one great heritage. The mosaic of South Asia's diverse cultures and religions, ranging from the largest segment of the Hindus, to the Muslims, the Buddhists, the Christians, the Sikhs and the Jains, has spread its influence far beyond the subcontinental periphery.

The white coastal beaches and blue lagoons of Maldives, the well designed tour gardens and Buddhist temples of Sri Lanka, the lush riverine beauty plus the sensuous arts of Bangladesh, the splendour of India's historical heritage and its architectural grandeur, epitomized by the Taj Mahal, the Mount Everest, and Kathmandu the city of antiquity of Nepal, the Karakoram ranges, archaeological wonders and imposing Mughal legacy at Lahore in Pakistan, make South Asia's garland full of colour and fragrance. Nature's bountiful gifts rub off its poor image due to poverty, unemployment, illiteracy and sporadic violence.

All these countries have suffered under the colonial and feudal governments for a long period of time. Even now this remains an unhappy legacy. India and Sri Lanka have exemplary record of democratic governance. But Pakistan and Bangladesh have suffered the rule under military dictatorships for a long period of time even after independence. Nepal and Bhutan are experimenting with democracy under liberal monarchy. Democracy is yet to take roots in Maldives.

These countries have suffered a great deal from communal and religious strife, in Sri Lanka between the Buddhist Sinhalese and Hindu Tamils, in India between Hindus and Muslims, in Pakistan between Shias and Sunnis on the one hand and the Punjabis or Pathans and Mohajirs (Migrants from India) on the other, in Bhutan between Lepchas and Nepalese, etc. Minorities have suffered a great deal in these countries as a result. The people of these countries have also faced insurgency and terrorism. The basic demographic indicators of the SAARC countries are summarized in Table 2.1

Table 2.1 : Basic Demographic Indicators of SAARC Countries

Country	Total Area In Sq. Km (000)	Population in million mid-1996 estimated	Urban Population (percent)*	Population in 1990 (million)	Projected in 2000 (million) estimated	Population in 2050 (million) estimated	Growth 1965-80 (%)	Growth 1980-90 (%)	Doubling Time (years)
Bangladesh	144.00	123.06	17.70	106.70	128	176	2.6	2.3	29.00
Bhutan	47.00	1.82	6.20	1.40	2	3	1.60	2.10	-
India	3287.60	952.11	26.50	849.50	1,006	1,348	2.30	2.10	34.00
Maldives	0.30	0.27	26.60	0.20	-	-	-	-	-
Nepal	140.80	22.09	13.10	18.90	24	37	2.40	2.60	28.00
Pakistan	803.90	129.27	34.10	112.40	147	240	3.10	3.10	23.00
Sri Lanka	65.60	18.55	22.10	17.00	19	24	1.80	1.40	48.00
Total	4486.60	1247.17	-	1106.10					

Source : Association of Indian Universities, New Delhi, *University News*, Vol. 36, No.19, May 11, 1998 , p.18.

* *Media Asia* an Asian Mass Communication Quarterly 24 (4) 1997.

The total area of the countries of the region is 4.487 million square kilometres or about one-tenth of Asia's total area of 44.3 million square kilometres. The population of the region was 1,106.1 million, about one-third of Asia's total population of 3,000 million in 1990-91. Urban population constituted slightly above one-fourth of the total population in the region. The population of the SAARC countries has been growing at the rate of more than 2 per cent every year, doubling itself in about 30 years time.

Countrywise Position

It may be useful here to briefly describe the socio-economic profile of each country before discussing the general problems and achievements in the region.

Bangladesh

Bangladesh is among the newest countries of South Asia. It is bounded on the west and north-west by West Bengal state of India, in north by Assam and Meghalaya states of India, on east by Assam and Tripura states of India and Myanmar (Burma). Bay of Bengal forms its southern border. Total land area of the country is 147,570 square kilometres and its population was about 111.4 million in 1991. Dhaka (6.951 million in 1991) is the capital of Bangladesh. Chittagong (2.348 million in 1991), Khulna (1.002 million in 1991) and Rajshahi (0.545 million in 1991) are the other important towns.

Bangladesh, formerly East Pakistan, became an independent entity in 1972, following the civil war under the leadership of Saikh Mujibur Rahman, who became its first Prime Minister. In January 1975 a presidential form of government replaced the parliamentary government and Saikh Mujibur Rahman became its President, assuming absolute powers. In August 1975 Saikh Mujibur Rahman and his family members were assassinated in a right wing coup led by a group of Islamic military officers. In November 1975 Major General Ziaur Rahman took over power and in June 1978, after general elections, he became its duly elected President. The political party set up by him, Bangladesh Nationalist Party (BNP), won 207 of the 300 seats in Jatiya Sangsad (National Parliament), providing the country temporary political stability. However, Major General Ziur Rahman was assassinated on 30th May 1981 and the political instability recurred. The elderly Vice President, Justice Abdus Sattar, who took over as acting President, faced strikes, demonstrations and even military coup and was forced to form a National Security Council under Lt. Gen. Hossain Mohammad Ershad in January 1882. Finally in a bloodless coup Justice Sattar was deposed and General Ershad took over as Chief Martial Law administrator. Suspending the constitution General Ershad assumed Presidency in December 1983.

In January 1986 General Ershad launched a political party, known as National Party, which won the majority of seats in Jatiya Sangsad in the general election of March 1986. General Ershad was re-elected President on 15th October 1986 and the Martial Law was lifted in November 1986. However, there was a popular uprising against the rule of General Ershad and he was deposed and arrested in December 1990. Mr. Shahabuddin Ahmad took over as acting President. Before the Twelfth Constitution Amendment Bill was passed in August 1991, there existed presidential form of government with a Prime Minister and council of ministers in subsidiary role under an elected president. Under the present system the prime minister with a council of ministers is vested with executive powers and the president, indirectly elected by the parliament, can only act on the advice of the prime minister. The Jatiya Sangsad is unicameral legislature with 300 elected seats, plus a further 30 seats reserved for women who are indirectly elected. But in the general election that followed, the Bangladesh National Party (BNP) of Begum Khalida Zia and Awami League of Sheikh Hasina Wazed emerged as large parties. Begam Khalida Zia, being the leader of the largest party became the Prime Minister. But soon thereafter the Bangladesh National Party was forced to organize fresh elections and was defeated by Awami League. In 1997 Saikh Hasina Wazed took over as Prime Minister and she ruled till 2001, when Begum Khalida Zia took over the reins of her party winning the majority of seats in general election.

Economy

Bangladesh is placed among the less developed countries of the world on account of low level of gross national product, low per capita income, US $ 259 in 1996, high density of population and high dependence on subsistence agriculture.

Its mineral resources include salt, limestone, white clay and glass sand. The total area under forests was 5.2 million acres (1986). Agriculture contributed 45.7 per cent of the GDP in 1986-87 and employed about 80 per cent of the economically active population. Bangladesh produced about 70 per cent of world's production of raw jute and, with a production of 1.2 million tons of jute goods (1987), this has been the principal foreign exchange earner. The coast line and the sea region of Bangladesh is suitable for fishing and there existed good potential for fish farming and fishing industry.

Large-scale industry is still not well established in Bangladesh. Major industries consisted of textile mills, jute mills, sugar factories, match factories, glass works, hosiery factories, paper mills and aluminium works. Due to poor management and market distortions its industrial structure has not grown and broadened over the years.

The economy of Bangladesh is dependent on imports for almost all essential goods, which included even food grains, while its exports base is narrow, effectively still reliant upon jute and jute products and tea. The main export commodities are jute goods, hides and skins, leather, tea, fish and fish products. Principal imports are machinery, transport equipment, manufactured goods, minerals and lubricants. With mounting imports bill and weak commodity exports the terms of trade have moved sharply against Bangladesh.

Economic policy and planning in Bangladesh have been significantly influenced by the demand of food grains from its rapidly expanding population. At the same time it has a very narrow natural resource base, which makes economic diversification difficult and have saddled the country with heavy trade deficit and dependence on foreign aid. The agriculture in Bangladesh suffered due to frequent floods and draught.

The country is in the process of transition from a predominantly agricultural economy to a modern economy. There have been significant shifts in the structure of the economy during the last two decades and the share of agriculture in the GDP has fallen from 55 per cent in 1970 to 32 per cent in 1995-96. Structural reforms have been undertaken to open new areas to private sector, deregulate private investment, relax exchange controls, reform business laws and down size the State Owned Enterprises (SOEs). Successive governments in Bangladesh have divested or denationalized industrial enterprises, banks and commercial business. The areas in which private entrepreneurs are being encouraged include tele-communication, postal services, radio broadcasting, telecasting and power plants.

The Industrial Policy of 1991 (revised in 1992) laid emphasis upon rapid industrial development of the country in terms of encouraging privatization, foreign investment and export-oriented industries. Industries have been opened to private investment, both local and foreign. Removing tariff barriers has liberalized imports. There has been simplification of procedures and reduction in tariff rates. The rates of direct taxes on individuals and also corporate tax have been reduced, apart from other tax reforms.

In Bangladesh Foreign Direct Investment (FDI) has been increasing steadily. Total FDI received by the country during 1995-96 was over US $ 900 million, which was 10 times the quantum in 1990-91. Malaysia, Japan, Hongkong, the UK, and India are among the top five investing countries. The total investments registered by the Board of Investment (BOI) between 1990-91 and 1994-95 amounted to US $ 2619 million. The main sectors in which this investment has taken place are textiles, services, chemicals, engineering, agro-based industries, glass and ceramics and food and allied industries.

Bhutan

The Kingdom of Bhutan, the land of the thunder dragon, lies in eastern Himalayas bordered on north by China and on all other sides by India. It has very high mountains, fertile valleys and thick forests. Tashichodzong, Thimpu is the administrative capital of Bhutan. Total land area of the country is 46,500 square kilometres and its population was about 0.6 million in 1991.

The first hereditary king of Bhutan, the Tongsa Penlop (the governor of the province of Tongsa in Central Bhutan) was installed on 17th December 1907. Sir Ugyen Wangchuk was elected the first hereditary Maharaja of Bhutan. The Bhutanese title was Druk Gyalpo. However, his successor is now addressed as King of Bhutan. Prior to 1907, initially Bhutan was ruled by a 'Dharmaraja' a person with spiritual authority whose successor was his re-incarnation. Later on the Lamas, who are religious priests, started electing a 'Devaraja', who jointly with the 'Dharmaraja' ruled the country. Both the spiritual authorities were responsible jointly to establish peace and order in the country. After the death of last Dharmaraja in 1903 there was no new reincarnation and with this the system of joint rule by two religious authorities, which was not working smoothly, was over. This created ground for hereditary kingship. The first King of Bhutan ruled from 1907 to 1928 and the second King from 1928 to 1952. Bhutan all along this period remained cut off from rest of the world. Roads were not constructed, no schools were opened and foreign tourists were seen with suspicion. In fact in 1958, when Pt. Jawaharlal Nehru, Prime Minister of India went to Bhutan on a state visit, there was no road connecting Bhutan with India.

An Anglo-Bhutanese Treaty signed in 1910, had placed Bhutan's foreign relations under the supervision of the Government of British India. After India became independent, the Treaty was replaced in August 1949 by a Indo-Bhutanese Treaty of Friendship, whereby Bhutan agreed to seek the advice of Government of India with regard to foreign relations, retaining freedom to decide whether or not to accept such an advice.

King Jigme Dorji Wangchuk, installed in 1952, established the National Assembly (Tshogdu) in 1953 and a Royal Advisory Council in 1965. He formed the country's first cabinet in May 1968. Dorji died in 1972 and was succeeded by the Western educated 16 year old Crown Prince Jigme Singye Wangchuk. The new King expressed his wish to maintain the Indo-Bhutanese Treaty of Friendship and to further strengthen the friendly relations with India.

When Chinese authority was established in Tibet in 1959, Bhutan had granted asylum to about 4,000 Tibetan refugees. By July 1960 most of these Tibetans had chosen Bhutanese citizenship and the remainder were accepted by India.

Bhutan joined the UN in 1971 and the Non-Aligned Movement in 1973. By 1987 Bhutan had established diplomatic relations with 13 countries, and maintained diplomatic missions at the UN, in New Delhi, in New York, in Dhaka, in Thailand and in Kathmandu.

In 1983 Bhutan became a founder member of the South Asian Association for Regional Co-operation (SAARC). In May 1985, Bhutan hosted the first meeting of ministers of foreign affairs from the SAARC countries. Bhutan hosted the next meeting of the heads of states of the SAARC countries in 1999.

Bhutan is a monarchy without a written constitution. From October 1969 the absolute monarchy was changed into democratic monarchy. The democracy in Bhutan, however, is different from the Western model, though an effort has been made to give representation to all regions and groups. There are no political parties. Bhutan followed the policy of democratic decentralization and had launched Dzonkhag Yargay Tshogchung (DYT) at district level in 1981 and further Geog Yargay Tshogchung (GYT) at block level in 1991. The representatives of these bodies attend National Assembly to represent their respective regions. Bhutan has 202 Geogs (Blocks). The DYTs and GYTs play an active role in the formulation and implementation of development programmes and in bringing forward the issues in the National Assembly. There is no adult franchise, no system of secret polling or direct elections. The members of the National Assembly are elected unanimously at the meetings of heads of families, which are presided over by District Collector. The National Assembly (Tshongdu), first instituted in 1953, has more than 200 members and meets twice a year. Two-third of the members of the National Assembly are elected by people for a term of three years. The central and the regional ecclesiastical bodies elect ten monastic representatives, while the remaining members are elected by the people. The King nominates the members of the Council of Ministers and the Royal Advisory Council.

Economy

Bhutan is among the underdeveloped countries of the world. Its economy is largely a subsistence economy based on small farming. Main agricultural crops are rice, millet, wheat, barley and maize. Cardamom, potatoes, oranges and apples are other agro-products. It has a large tract of forests. The livestock includes cattle, yak, pig, sheep, goat and poultry. The Kingdom's Gross National Product (GNP), and per capita income at US $ 415 in 1995, was the lowest among the SAARC countries.

As per geological investigations there are large deposits of limestone, marble, dolomite, graphite, lead, copper, slate, coal, talc, gypsum, beryl, mica, pyrites and tufa in Bhutan. However, commercial viability of the mineral deposits has not been tested. For mineral exploration and exploitation Bhutan has taken the help of Geological Survey of India.

Trade in commodities in the past was done through barter, which is now gradually shifting to market. India is Bhutan's major trading partner. Timber, cardamom and liquor are exported to Middle East, Singapore, Western Europe and other parts of the world.

In 1987 there were about 400 small scale and cottage industry units besides a cement plant, a food processing plant, a tea chest ply veneer factory, a resin and turpentine factory, a salt iodination plant and three distilleries.

There are two banks in Bhutan, namely the Bank of Bhutan (BOB) and the Bhutan National Bank (BNB). The Bank of Bhutan was established in 1968 with its headquarter at Phuntsholing with 22 branches throughout the country. The Bhutan National Bank established in 1996 has its headquarter at Thimpu. For insurance business, Bhutan has Royal Insurance Corporation of Bhutan (RICB), having its head office at Phuntsholing. Business entrepreneurs have formed Bhutan Chamber of Commerce and Industry (BC&I), to discuss and resolve their common problems.

Bhutan has good potential for hydropower generation. It had completed Chhukha Power Project in 1988 with the help of India. The Sankosh Hydro Electric Project initiated in 1993 is under construction. Besides irrigation it is expected to produce 1,125 Megawatt electricity. It supplies the surplus electricity to India under the agreement.

For economic development Bhutan had adopted planning. The First Five-Year Plan was initiated in 1961. Since then it has completed seven five-year plans. The National Council approved the Eighth Five-Year Plan on 16th July 1997.

Thus Bhutan is a land locked country, isolated geographically, with extremely mountainous terrain, limited agricultural land, widely scattered population living in remote areas and limited roads and communication network. Its economy is linked with the Indian economy, with 80 per cent of its trade with India. Agriculture, the mainstay of its economy, is based on subsistence farming. This limited the ability of the government to raise domestic revenue. Obviously Bhutan has to rely upon external assistance for funding its development programmes.

Gradually the economy is changing, though the growth of private investment is slow due to the lack of local entrepreneurship and rudimentary financial markets. Some policy changes have been made recently. The Companies Act of the Kingdom of Bhutan, 1989 was passed to facilitate corporatisation of public sector enterprises and privatize wherever possible. Establishment of small scale and medium sized industries is being encouraged. Financial incentives are given for setting up industries etc. All these indications are good for the future.

India

India the seventh largest country in the world and the second largest in Asia occupies a strategic position in South Asia, looking across the seas to Arabia and Africa on the west and to Burma, Malaysia and Indonesia on the east. Mighty Himalayas separate India from the countries of Central Asia like Tibet, China, Russia, and Afghanistan. All other countries of South Asia are situated on India's periphery, Nepal and Bhutan on the north, Bangladesh on the east, Pakistan on the west and Sri Lanka and Maldives on the south.

India lies on north of Equator between 8° 4′ and 37° 6′ north latitudes and 68° 7′ and 97° 25′ east longitudes. It is bounded on the southwest by the Arabian Sea and on the southeast by Bay of Bengal. On north, northeast and northwest lie the Himalayan ranges extending practically uninterrupted for a distance of about 2,500 km. The Indian Ocean washes its southern tip.

India measures 3,214 km. from north to south and 2,933 km. from east to west, with a total land area of 32,87,263 square kilometres. It has land frontier of 15,200 km. and a coastline of 7,516.5 km. Andaman and Nicobar Islands in the Bay of Bengal and Lakshadweep islands in the Arabian Sea are part of India. All major landforms, hills, mountains, plateau, plains, are well represented in India. There are extensive plains suitable for agriculture and washed by a river system flowing from Himalayas and other mountain ranges.

New Delhi is capital of India. Other important cities are Mumbai (Bombay – population 12.6 million in 1991), Kolkata (Calcutta – population 11.0 million in 1991), Delhi (population 8.5 million in 1991), Chennai (Madras – population 5.4 million in 1991), Hyderabad (population 4.3 million in 1991), Bangalore (population 4.1 million in 1991) and Ahmedabad (population 3.3 million in 1991).

According to 1991 census, India's population was 84,39,30,861, among which 43,75,97,929 were males and 40,63,32,932 females. The growth in population between 1901 and 1991 was 254 per cent and between 1981 and 1991 was 23.50 per cent. The decadal growth rate went up from 5.75 per cent between 1901 and 1911 to 23.50 per cent between 1981 and 1991. The average exponential growth rate increased from 0.56 per cent between 1901 to 1911 to 2.11 per cent between 1981 and 1991.

The sex ratio in India has always been in favour of males, from 972 females per 1,000 males in 1901 to 929 females per 1,000 males in 1991. Further there has been successive decline in sex ratio since 1901, except for the census of 1951 and 1981, when it showed a marginal rise.

Major religious communities in India are Hindus 82.64 per cent, Muslims 11.35 per cent, Christians 2.43 per cent, Sikhs 1.96 per cent, Buddhists 0.71 per cent and Jains 0.48 per cent.

The demographic situation in India is not conducive to development. It has high concentration of population in a small area and not uniformly distributed all over, with higher concentration in Indo-Gangatic plain, coastal areas and urban areas. Moreover the density is continuously rising sharply resulting in breakdown of urban services like electricity, sewerage disposal etc. Socio-political institutions like caste and religion dominate an average Indian's life and determine his social status and career potential. Nonetheless unity of Indian cultural heritage has acted as a strong cohesive force. The demographic and economic information about India is given in Table 2.2.

Though nothing can be written with certainty, as per historical records the period of Aryan migration and settlement in the west of India is estimated around 1500 BC. Composition of Rig Veda was the high watermark of the period. From here they migrated to other parts of the country. The Mahabharat War occurred in 900 BC. Upanishads, a set of religious scriptures of Hindus, were composed around 550 BC. There was a religious renaissance around this time with the preachings of

Budha and Mahaveer. The approximate date of Bhudha's nirvana is taken as 544 BC.

Table 2.2 : Demographic and Economic Statistics of India

	1950-51	1960-61	1970-71	1980-81	1990-91	1994-95
Demographic :						
Population (million)	361.1	439.2	548.2	683.3	846.3	915.9
Birth Rate (per 000)	39.9	41.7	41.2	37.2	29.5	28.3
Death Rate (per 000)	27.4	22.8	19.0	15.0	9.8	9.0
Expectation of Life						
Males (years)	32.4	41.9	46.9	50.9	55.9	61.9
Females (years)	31.7	40.6	44.7	50.0	55.9	63.1
Medical and Health:						
Hospitals (No.)	2,694	3,094	3,862	8,804	11,174	N. A.
Dispensaries (No.)	6,515	9,406	12,180	16,751	27,431	N. A.
Primary Health Centres	725	2,565	5,112	5,740	20,450	21,536
Number of Beds	117	230	349	569	811	N. A.
National Income:						
GDP at Current Prices (Rs. Crores)	8,979	15,254	39,708	122,427	477,814	854,103
1980-81Prices (Rs. Cr.)	42,871	62,904	90,426	122,427	213,983	251,010
Per Capita Income:						
Current Prices (Rs.)	238.8	328.2	674.7	1630.1	4983.0	8281.5
1980-81 Prices (Rs.)	1126.9	1350.3	1519.6	1630.1	2222.2	2449.2

N.A. : Not available

Source : India Abstract 1997, Directorate of Audio Visual & Publicity, Government of India, August 1997.

With prosperity many invaders were attracted to India. Among these Alexandra the Great invaded India in 326 BC, Ashok the Great reigned during the period 272 to 232 BC, Mohammed Bin Kassim invaded Sind in 711 AD and Muhammad Ghori defeated Prithviraj Chouhan in 1192. Babur defeated the Lodis and established Mughal Empire in 1526. Akbar the Great ruled between 1556 and 1605. In the mean time Vasco da Gama had landed at Calicut in 1498. The Portuguese captured Goa in 1510. The East India Company was constituted in 1600. In 1602 the Netherlands East India Company was constituted. The Dutch opened a factory at Pulicut in 1609 and the English traders built a factory at Musalipatnam in 1611. Then followed a phase of consolidation of trading contacts with the country. Gradually these traders developed interest in governance of small-unorganized states. In 1748 the first Anglo-French War was fought and in 1757 English defeated Siraja- u-Daulah – Mir Jafar the Nawab of Bengal, at the Battle of Plassey. In 1764 English defeated Mir Kasim at the Battle of Butar and in 1767-69, they defeated Hyder Ali of Mysore. Finally, in 1772 Warren Hastings became the Governor of Bengal. Thus British, who to begin with had settled in the coastal areas for trading, gradually spread their hold over many parts of the country. They maintained troops and manipulated the feudal order to their advantage.

People resented the activities of the British and the First war for independence was fought in 1857 against the aliens. This provided the British crown an opportunity to take over the Indian Government through Royal Proclamation. However, the desire for independence was seething in the hearts of Indian people. In 1885 the Indian National Congress, with Shri W.C. Banerjee as President, was formed to unite the patriotic elements and strive for country's independence. A struggle for independence was fought with British for almost 80 years under the banner of Indian National Congress under the leadership of Bal Gangadhar Tilak, Lala Lajpat Rai, Mahatma Gandhi, Pandit Jawaharlal Nehru and others.

India gained freedom from British with the proclamation of independence on 15th August 1947. India became a Sovereign, Socialist, Secular, and Democratic Republic, under the Constitution adopted on 16th November 1949, which came into effect on 26th January 1950. The Constitution granted six fundamental rights to a citizen, viz., Right of Equality, Right of Freedom, Right against Exploitation, Right to Freedom of Religion, Cultural and Educational Rights and Right to Constitutional Remedies. The Constitution of India provides it a unitary as well as federal character. In the Union at the apex there is a President, Executive Head of State, elected by an electoral college consisting of elected members of both Houses of Parliament and Legislative Assemblies of the States, and a Vice President elected by members of both Houses of Parliament. The government at the centre consists of a Council of Ministers headed by a Prime Minister. The Parliament for the

Union is bi-cameral, with the House of People (Lok Sabha) consisting of members elected directly through adult franchise, and Council of States (Rajya Sabha) consisting of elected representatives of States.

There are 32 States and 7 Union Territories. Each State has one or two houses of Legislature. The Legislative Assembly consists of members elected through adult franchise with a Chief Minister and Council of Ministers, to advise the Governor who is head of the State. A Lieutenant Governor or an Administrator administers the union territories. All the executive powers are exercised by the President on the advice of the Council of Ministers responsible to the Parliament.

Economy

Soon after independence India embarked upon planned development. The first five-year plan was initiated in 1951. With nine five-year plans and three one-year plans India's achievements have been significant. Considering the private per capita average real consumption growth over 1990-95 required to halve the incidence of poverty, using US $ 1 per day international poverty line and no income distribution changes, India is one of the few countries which have seen relatively faster growth.

India's achievements in agriculture have been significant. With improved irrigation, fertilizers, double cropping and high yielding variety it not only met the increased requirement of the increasing population but also contributed to export earnings by raising cash crops like cotton, jute, tea, sugarcane, coffee etc. Despite India's remarkable technical expertise agriculture continues to provide living for a vast majority of people, particularly in rural areas. There has been a marked shift in economic emphasis away from farm sector to industry and service sector over the last fifty years.

There exists high degree of economic duality in India with its achievements in the field of technology spanning nuclear power, satellite communication, manufacture of silicon chips and most sophisticated arms and ammunition including warships and fighter aircrafts on the one hand and small industries and rural crafts based on low level antiquated traditional technology and caloric deficient poor masses in rural areas on the other. Moreover since independence India's economic development has been deeply rooted in centralized planning with regulation of private sector, widespread public ownership and tight control of trade and capital flows. The regulatory framework, however, started loosening under Rajiv Gandhi and has been further liberalized by the governments following him.

Over the years foreign trade has been progressively under-emphasized, as economic development proceeded along the path of import substitution and behind the protective walls. This undermined industrial efficiency and positively debarred agricultural improvements. It was during the last decade that a better appreciation and efforts to push exports to meet the country's requirement of foreign exchange for the import of technology and capital goods, petroleum products and essential raw materials has emerged. However, the pattern of exports has not changed significantly and there has always remained a trade deficit, which has to be met out of repatriation of savings of NRIs, foreign aid and investment by FIIs.

To provide thrust to key areas of economy including industry, government has provided tax benefits, and incentives for exports, Non-Resident Indians and specified industries. A variety of incentives are further provided by the state governments, such as investment subsidy, tax breaks, exemption/deferment of specific duties etc.

Policy changes were initiated in 1991 to attract private investment as well as significant capital inflows into India on a sustained basis and to encourage technology collaboration agreements. Changes in trade policies included a significant scaling down of tariff barriers, virtual dismantling of the system of imports and export licences and simplification of procedures. Tax structure has been rationalized and customs and excise duties have been reduced. Besides simplification the rates of tax for individuals and companies have been reduced. Treaties have been formalized with over 40 countries for double taxation relief.

Foreign investment has grown as a result. The total investment in 1995-96 was around US $ 4077 million, which was shared almost equally by direct investment and portfolio investment. The main sectors in which this investment has taken place are electronics and electric machinery, services, chemicals, non-electric machinery, food and agro-processing. The countries making investment included Mauritius, the USA, Hongkong, Singapore, Germany, Japan and the UK.

India's total trade with the SAARC countries in 1994 was US $ 1132 million, of which US $ 1002 million were exports and US $ 130 million were imports. However, as a proportion of trade with the world, which stood at US $ 49.13 billion in 1994, the trade with the SAARC countries was only 2.3 per cent. Bangladesh, Sri Lanka and Pakistan are India's main trading partners among the SAARC countries. India forms a major source of imports into Nepal and Bhutan. Under SAPTA India has opened up with its neighbours trade negotiations and has given them a variety of concessions and preferences in trade and investment.

Maldives

The Republic of Maldives (Divehi Jumburiya), a country of islands, is situated at a distance of about 675 km. south-west of Sri Lanka, in the Indian Ocean. It consists of more than 1,190 small coral islands. Out of these only 202 are inhabited. With land area of 0.30 (000) square km. and population of 0.20 million (1991), Maldives is the smallest among the member countries of SAARC. For the purpose of administration Maldives is divided into the Capital, Male and 19 other administrative districts (one each for one Atoll), each under an appointed governor (Verin), assisted by local chiefs (Katheebum) who are also appointed.

Maldives was known as Maldives Islands until April 1969, with an elected Sultan as head of state. It was placed under British protection, with internal self-government, in 1887. It became a republic in January 1953. The Sultanate was restored in February 1954. Maldives became an independent country, outside the British Commonwealth, on 26th July 1965. Following a referendum, the republic was established again in November 1968, with Ibrahim Nasir, who was Prime Minister since 1954, as President.

In 1956 the Maldivian government permitted the establishment of a Royal Air Force staging post on Gan, an island in the southern most Atoll, Addu. In 1975 British Government's decision to close down the base and to evacuate British forces created a military void in the region and economic problems for Maldives. In October 1977 President Nasir, however, rejected the offer from the USSR to lease the former base on Gan for annual payment of US $ 1 million, announcing that he would not lease the island for military purposes, nor lease it to a super power.

In March 1975 President Nasir dismissed Prime Minister Ahmed Zaki and abolished the post of Prime Minister. Maumoon Abdul Gayoom, Minister of Transport was approved through a referendum in July 1978 as President to succeed President Nasir, who did not stand for the post. President Gayoom got re-elected for afresh term of 5 years in September 1983, September 1988, September 1993, and September 1998 and is continuing as President. A coup attempted in November 1988 by certain political elements with the help of Sri Lankan mercenaries was foiled with the timely help from India.

In Maldives the legislative power is vested in a unicameral Citizens' Council (Majlis) with 48 members, while the executive power is vested in the President, elected by popular vote or nominated by the Majlis for a period of 5 years. The President governs with the help of a Cabinet appointed by him and responsible to the Majlis. There are no political parties.

Economy

Most of the people in Maldives live on tiny coral islands in scattered Atolls covered with coconut palms. The main products of the islands are millet, cassava, yams, melons, tropical fruits and coconut.

The islanders have for long remained outside the money economy, subsisting by fishing and collecting coconut. Earlier rats destroyed a large proportion of coconut crop so a massive programme to destroy the rats had to be taken up in 1981.

Maldives has shown better achievement compared to that of other South Asian countries. During 1970s the increase in country's population averaged 3 per cent annually while the average annual rate of economic growth was 8.9 per cent between 1976 and 1986, largely as a result of increased revenue from fishing and tourism. Between 1965 and 1985 there was an average increase in per capita gross national product (GNP) of 1.9 per cent per annum. Maldives' per capita GNP at US $ 900 (1996) was the highest among the SAARC countries.

Fisheries are the key sector in the Maldivian economy, contributing around 15 per cent to its GDP. Tuna fish accounted for around 85 per cent of total catch, 65 per cent of which was exported. Dried/frozen skipjack, tuna and canned fish accounted for about 85 per cent of total export earnings in 1995. Mechanical boats are now gradually replacing the traditional boats (dhonis).

Tourism is the other mainstay of the economy of Maldives. White sandy beaches and multi-coloured coral formations are main attractions for tourists. Introduced in 1972, when the first tourist resort was set up, tourism is growing at a fast rate and in 1994 there were 73 operating tourist resorts. In 1994, the total number of tourists visiting Maldives was more than 275,000, which equalled the country's population. The tourist arrivals have been growing at the rate of 16 per cent per annum. The bulk of the tourists come from Europe (69%) and Asia (25%). The contribution of tourism to government revenue was 33 per cent and to GDP 18.4 per cent in 1995.

Maldives imports most of the essential consumer and capital goods. In 1985 imports amounted to US $ 47.9 million and exports to US $ 23 million, of which about 29 per cent were to Thailand, 24 per cent to the USA and 20 per cent to Sri Lanka. Exports from Maldives stood at US $ 49.6 million and the imports at US $ 235 million in 1994-95. The bulk of the Maldives' imports are from Singapore (36%), UAE, India, Sri Lanka, Hong Kong and Japan. The countries to which Maldives exports its goods are Sri Lanka, the UK, the USA, Germany, Japan and Thailand. Thus except for Sri Lanka and India, which together constituted 18 per cent of Maldives' trade, trade with other SAARC countries was negligible. Fish and coconut have been its main export commodities.

The Ministry of Trade and Industry together with the Foreign Investment Services Bureau (FISB) is responsible for dealing with the legal and administrative set up for planning, implementing and managing the activities of trade and investment. Law provides for foreign investment guarantee and repatriation of profits. It establishes guidelines covering the duration of investment, applicability of immigration charges, dispute settlement and royalty charges. Foreign investors can enter through partnerships with local entrepreneurs or as sole proprietors.

The package of incentives offered to foreign investors includes long-term tax holiday, free currency conversion, custom duty exemption on import of materials and equipment for business etc. All this opens up possibility of growth of industry, trade, banking etc. in future.

Nepal

The Kingdom of Nepal (Nepal Adhirajya) is a land locked Asian country situated in Himalayan mountain ranges, extending from 26° 20′ to 30° 10′ north and 80° 15′ to 88° 15′ east. It is bound on north by Tibet, on east by Sikkim and West Bengal state of India, on south and west by Bihar and Uttar Pradesh states of India. There are 3 geographical regions in which the country is divided, viz., the fertile Tarai plains in the south, the belts containing Mahabharat Lekh and Churia Hills and basins of inner Tarai at the centre and the Himalayan region in the north. Total area of Nepal is 147,181 square km. and population was 18.49 million in 1991. Administratively Nepal is divided into 5 development regions, 14 zones and 75 districts.

Kathmandu (population 0.32 million in 1990) is the capital of Nepal. Other important cities are Patan (population 0.248 million in 1990), Biratnagar (population 0.210 million in 1990) and Bhaktapur (population 0.118 million in 1990).

Nepal was earlier a group of petty principalities. The inhabitants of one of that, the Gurkhas, became dominant in 1769. From 1846 to 1951 a family of hereditary Rana Prime Ministers in the name of King ruled Nepal in effect. The Rana Prime Ministers pursued a policy of close cooperation with

British power in India. The Nepali Congress Party, in late 1940s, started a movement for democratic government. This led to a revolution, the autocratic Rana Prime Ministers were thrown out and King Tribhuwan, who earlier was only a titular King, assumed power. In the first democratic elections in 1959 an overwhelming majority voted the Nepali Congress Party to power. However, in 1960 King Mahendra, who succeeded King Tribhuwan, dismissed the government and the Parliament and introduced a system of guided democracy named Partyless Panchayat system.

King Birendra, who became King in February 1975 on the death of King Mahendra, conducted a national referendum on 2nd May 1980. This produced a narrow mandate for the continuation of Partyless Panchayat system with democratic reforms. Accordingly democratic reforms and decentralisation of powers were initiated. In April 1990, the King dissolved the 46 months old Council of Ministers and appointed Lokendra Bahadur Chand as Prime Minister. However, the bloody clashes that followed the all-party agitation for democracy led to dissolution of National Panchayat and formation of a United Front government led by Nepal Congress leader Krishna Prasad Bhattarai. In the general elections held in 1991 the Nepal Congress was returned to power again and a government led by M.P. Koirala was formed. In the general elections held in 1999, the Nepal Congress was returned to power for the third time with a massive majority.

His Majesty the King of Nepal is the symbol of Nepalese nationality and unity of people. The executive powers are vested in His Majesty and the Council of Ministers headed by the Prime Minister. His Majesty appoints the leader of the party that commands majority in the House of Representatives, Prime Minister. Other ministers are appointed on the recommendation of the Prime Minister from among the members of parliament. The Council of Ministers is answerable to Parliament. The Parliament is bicameral, comprising of the House of Representatives with 205 members and the National Council with 60 members. The tenure of office of members of the House of Representatives is five years and that of National Council six years.

Nepal has very close ethnic and cultural relations with India. Its economy has been largely dependent on India. Before 1947 there existed a Treaty of Trade and Transit with the Government of British India. A treaty on similar lines was signed with the Government of India in 1951. It was further extended from time to time, for providing special status to Nepal in respect of its trade and transit through India. In 1978 two separate treaties, one for trade and the other for transit replaced it, which were further renewed in 1983 and 1984. There was some delay in further renewal of the Treaty. This caused hardship to the people of both the countries. In 1987, therefore, a Joint Commission for the promotion of economic cooperation between the two countries was set up. Finally, the dispute was resolved and in 1990 a new Treaty was signed.

Nepal has also maintained good relations with China. China also contributed to Nepalese economy in a significant way. Both the countries have maintained close political and economic relations. Nepal has also maintained close trade and economic relations with Bangladesh, which provided it an alternate transit route for import and export trade with other countries.

Nepal has been a part of non-aligned movement and maintained diplomatic relations with 99 countries in 1987. It is also a founder member of the South Asian Association for Regional Cooperation. The Secretariat of the SAARC is located at Kathmandu, the capital of Nepal. It is also member of the United Nations.

Economy

Due to inhospitable terrain, comprising of isolated valleys, very high mountains and bitter climatic conditions in some of the parts, Nepal is among the least developed countries of the world. Forests cover a large tract of its land and in 1981 about 91 per cent of the people were engaged in agriculture, forestry and fishing. Primary sector contributed about 59 per cent to its gross national product and about 60 per cent to export earnings. Industry contributed about 10 per cent, 6 per cent by traditional cottage and small-scale industries and 4 per cent by modern industries. Nepal's per capita income at US $ 200 in 1995 placed it among the 12 poor countries of the world. The gross national product grew at an average rate of 2.3 per cent in real terms. In 1995-96 the GDP at factor cost (at current prices) reflected a growth of 6.1 per cent over the previous year.

Agriculture is the predominant sector of the Nepalese economy contributing over 40 per cent of the GDP and providing employment to 80 per cent of the people. The main crops include paddy, maize, wheat, barley and millets. However, gradually the share of agriculture in GDP is falling.

Manufacturing accounted for less than 10 per cent of Nepal's GDP and provided employment to only 3 per cent of the total labour force in the country. Major industries are food, beverages, tobacco, textiles, leather products, cement and bricks. Most of these industries are located in the Tarai region.

Tourism including tracking and rafting is the major foreign exchange earning industry. It contributed 21.6 per cent of total foreign exchange earnings of 1994-95. About 320,000 tourists arrived in Nepal, one-third of which were from the SAARC countries and largest number from India.

Nepal Rastra Bank is the central bank of Nepal. There are 10 commercial banks including 5 foreign banks and 2 development banks. A Securities Exchange Market and a Securities Exchange Board were also set up some years back.

The rivers of Nepal are considered suitable for generation of hydroelectric power. However, it was estimated that in 1986 only 0.05 per cent of the potential was exploited. As per geological survey reports Nepal has significant deposits of lignite, copper, cobalt, magnetite and zinc. However, their commercial viability has not been established and the mineral resources have remained unexploited.

India has been Nepal's major trading partner with 44 per cent share in exports and 40 per cent share in imports in 1986-87. Almost the entire trade of Nepal passed through India. For China-Nepal trade there existed 21 trade routes along the border in north. Important items of trade are textiles, salt, petrol, kerosene oil, sugar, medicines, paper, cement, iron and steel and tea. Gradually Nepal is also building trade relations with the USA, Japan, European Union and East Asian countries.

Nepal has adopted a liberal market driven trade policy and the thrust has been towards the reduction in trade imbalance through exports promotion, establishment of Export Processing Zones, creation of better communication infrastructure and improved imports management. The broad, open and liberal Industrial Policy of 1992, provided encouragement to private sector in all sectors of economy.

Foreign investment in Nepal is regulated by the Foreign Investment and Technology Transfer Act, 1992. Foreign investment up to 100 per cent equity is permitted. Technology transfers are welcome. Full repatriation of funds including equity, profits, dividends, interest on loan funds is allowed. Several incentives are provided to industries. These initiatives are reshaping the economy of Nepal from traditional to modern.

Pakistan

The Islamic Republic of Pakistan is a federation of four provinces, viz., Punjab, Sind, Baluchistan and North-West Frontier Province. Extending from 28° 45′ to 36° 50′ north and between 60° 55′ and 75° 30′ east, it is bounded on north-west by Iran and Afghanistan, on north by Tajikistan (former USSR) and China, on east by India and on south by the Arabian Sea. The total land area of Pakistan is 8,03,900 square km. and its population was 112.40 million in 1991. It is a Muslim majority state, with about 96.68 per cent of its population being Muslims, as per the 1991 census. A Minorities Wing has been, however, set up at the Religious Affairs Ministry to safeguard the constitutional rights of religious minorities, which consist of Hindus (1.5 %), Christians (1.6 %), Parsees, Budhists and others.

Islamabad is the capital of Pakistan. Other major towns are, Karachi (population 5.1 million in 1991), Lahore (population 2.920 million in 1991), Faisalabad (population 1.090 million in 1991), Rawalpindi (population 0.920 in 1991) and Hyderabad (population 0.795 million in 1991).

A separate state for Muslims of the Indian subcontinent was set up by the British on the argument that Muslims by virtue of their religion and cultural distinction constituted a separate nation. Poet philosopher Muhammad Iqbal had articulated the concept of a separate state comprising of Muslim majority areas in northwestern India. The All India Muslim League led by Muhammad Ali Jinnah adopted the concept in 1940 and the dream of Pakistan came into existence on partition of British India on 14th August 1947. Pakistan, a country divided into two parts separated by a distance of more than 1000 kilometres, existed upto March 1971, when East Pakistan became Bangladesh.

Pakistan has a history of military dominating civil administration and Generals dismissing the democratically elected governments and seizing power. Pakistan was proclaimed Islamic Republic on 23 March 1956 with federal parliamentary form of government. But Field Marshall Ayub Khan seized power in a coup in October 1958 and proclaimed presidential system in the Constitution of 1962. General Yahya Khan deposed Ayub in March 1969.

In the first free elections in December 1970 Zulfikar Ali Bhutto's Pakistan Peoples' Party won majority of seats in the western half, while Sheikh Mujibar Rahman's Awami League swept the polls in the eastern half, winning 160 of the 162 seats and securing a controlling majority in the National Assembly. However, Bhutto refused to sit in opposition and allow Mujib to form government. This created a rift among the people of two parts. Mujib raised the demand of autonomy for East Pakistan, which was rejected by Bhutto and General Yahya Khan. Mujib was arrested and put behind the bars. The repression of people that followed led to mass exodus of Hindus and others from East Pakistan to India, causing avoidable burden on the economy and polity of India. The civil war that followed resulted in intervention by India, defeat and surrender of about 1 lakh Pakistani troops before Indian Army and finally, in the proclamation of Peoples' Republic of Bangladesh on 26th March 1971.

General Yahaya Khan handed over the power to the civilian government led by Z.A. Bhutto, who ruled West Pakistan until July 1977 when he was deposed and executed by General Zia Ul Haq, who took over the power and ruled until he was killed in a plane crash on August 17, 1988. Senate Chairman Ghulam Ishaq

Khan took over as acting President and the country was placed under emergency rule.

In the general elections held on November 16, 1988 the Pakistan Peoples' Party led by Benazir Bhutto won the largest number of seats and became Prime Minister on December 9, 1988 and Ghulam Ishaq Khan became President on December 12, 1988. However, Ghulam Ishaq Khan fell out with Benazir Bhutto, dismissed her government, dissolved the National Assembly and ordered fresh elections on August 8, 1990. Islamic Jamhoori Ittehad Party under Nawaz Sharief won the majority of seats and he became Prime Minister in November 1990. The Pakistan Peoples' Party led by Benazir Bhutto was returned to power again in 1993 but was dismissed by the President on charges of corruption. The Parliament was dissolved and fresh elections were held. In the subsequent elections held in 1998 the Islamic Jamhori Ittehad Party won the majority of seats and Nawaz Sharief became Prime Minister once again.

The 1973 Constitution, which though has been substantially amended since then, provides for a federal democratic structure with president as head of State to act on the advice of the Prime Minister. The Federal Legislature consists of the Lower House, called National Assembly with 207 members elected directly for a period of five years plus 10 members representing minorities, and the Upper House called the Senate with 87 members who serve for six years, with one-third retiring every two years.

There is a high degree of religious homogeneity in Pakistan with about 96.7 per cent of the people being Muslims. However, people in general have suffered due to inter-sectoral feuds between Shias and Sunnis, Punjabis and Mohajirs, etc.

Pakistan is member of the United Nations, the Commonwealth, the Colombo Plan, and the South Asian Association for Regional Cooperation. Pakistan has received massive military assistance from the USA under the Mutual Defence Assistance Agreement signed on 19th May 1954.

Economy

The western part of Pakistan is mountainous while the north is covered by high mountain ranges with snow clad peaks.

However, the rest of the country has fertile plains irrigated by Sindhu and its four tributaries. With per capita income of US $ 480 Pakistan is relatively better off among the SAARC countries, except for Maldives and Sri Lanka. The Indus Water Treaty of 1960 between India and Pakistan provided a basis of development programmes funded by the World Bank and other developed countries. Agriculture including forestry and fishing is the mainstay of Pakistan's economy, employing about 51 per cent of the working population and contributing 23.7 per cent to gross domestic product (GDP). The main crops are rice, wheat, cotton, maize and sugar cane. Pakistan is self-sufficient in food.

In 1985-86 Pakistan had 106,580 km. of roads of which 45,686 km. were all weather roads. In 1986-87 Pakistan Railways had tracks covering 8,775 km. served 83 million passengers and carried 11.6 million tons of freight. There are international airports at Lahore, Karachi and Islamabad. Pakistan is served by many international airlines, besides its national carrier Pakistan Airways.

Pakistan had no industries worth the name at the time of independence. Gradually a base was prepared and it is growing. Industries employed about 10 per cent of the population and contributed about one-fifth to the GDP in 1987-88. Main industries are sugar, vegetable products, jute textiles, soda ash, sulphuric acid, caustic soda, paper and paperboards, bicycles, cotton textiles, cement, steel etc. Main items of export are cotton cloth, cotton yarn, rice, leather, carpets and tapestries.

Pakistan has substantial coal reserves. But only a part of it is exploited. The power availability has been low, making it dependent on petrol and diesel imports. The Himalayan Hill stations, magnificent scenarios and its salubrious climate provide excellent opportunity for field sports, mountaineering and winter sports in Pakistan. These places also attract large number of tourists from different parts of the country and also from foreign countries.

Low investment and savings ratios, low agricultural productivity and heavy fuel imports burden have been the principal constraints to economic growth. Dependence of agriculture on weather (monsoon) is another serious structural shortcoming.

The export base of Pakistan being narrow its export performance has been erratic with heavy dependence on cotton and rice, despite some degree of diversification. Country's dependence on oil imports has forced it to foster closure links with the oil producers in Middle East.

Pakistan's trade with the SAARC countries is not substantial. In fact the exports to the SAARC countries amounted only to 3.4 per cent of the total exports of Pakistan, while imports from the SAARC countries amounted to 1.4 per cent. Among these countries India, Bangladesh and Sri Lanka are its main trade partners.

Pakistan has an outward looking industrial strategy, providing an environment highly conducive to investment, by both domestic and foreign entrepreneurs. Private investment is being encouraged in all types of manufacturing activities as well as vital sectors, such as energy, transport, communication, fertilizers, cement and social services.

The policy announced in 1994 has made privatization programme in industry broad based. Privatization is also being encouraged in banking. Special incentives are provided to investors setting up enterprises in Export Processing Zones (EPZs). With higher growth in manufacturing, services and agriculture and increase in investment activity the GDP has grown at 6.1 per cent during 1995-96.

Sri Lanka

Known to the ancient world as Taprobane and later on as Serendip, the island was known as Lanka, Sinhala Deepa and Seelan during different times. In 1972 it was given its present name Sri Lanka. The Democratic Socialist Republic of Sri Lanka comprises of one large island (435 km. from north to south and 225 km. from east to west) and several islets, lying east of the southern tip of the Indian subcontinent. The Bay of Bengal lies to its north and east and the Arabian Sea to its west. The Gulf of Mannar and the Palk Strait with shallow water and a chain of islands linking *Sri Lanka and India separate Sri Lanka from India.* Total land area of Sri Lanka is 64,454 square km.

and its population was 17 million in 1990, with the lowest rate of growth at 1.4 per cent among the SAARC countries.

Sri Jayawardenapura is the administrative and Colombo the commercial capital of Sri Lanka. Colombo (population 0.615 million in 1990), Dehiwala-Mount Lavinia (population 0.193 million in 1990), Moratuwa (population 0.170 million in 1990), Jaffna (population 0.129 million in 1990) and Kandy (population 0.104 million in 1990) are other important towns.

Budhism, introduced from India in the 3rd century BC, is the main religion of its people. About 74 per cent of the inhabitants are Buddhists Sinhalese. Hindu Tamils are the second largest group forming about 18 per cent of its total population. The two communities are divided on linguistic as well as religious lines.

Among the European traders the Portugese were the first to reach Sri Lanka at the beginning of the 16th century. They settled on the West Coast and converted many of the inhabitants to Christianity. One hundred years later they were replaced by the Dutch, who occupied most of the coastal region, only the kingdom of Kandy in the centre of the country retained its independence. The British, to whom Candy surrendered in 1815, evicted the Dutch. The country regained its independence on 4th February 1948. On 22nd May 1948 Sri Lanka became a republic.

A youth insurrection in April 1971 rocked Prime Minister Sirimao Bandaranaike's United Front government and finally, in 1977 general elections she was swept out of power by the United National Party. Prime Minister Junius Jayawardane replaced the 1972 Constitution and became President and the Prime Minister both. In 1988 former Prime Minister Ranasinhe Premadasa was elected Executive President.

There has been a strong demand from the Tamils of Sri Lanka for greater autonomy and power. Tamil United Liberation Front spearheaded the movement. Later on a more militant organisation, Liberation Tigers of Tamil Eelam (LTTE) took the initiative for a separate Tamil state. They could mobilize the youth and took to violent struggle for the cause. There have been bloody encounters between the Tigers and the Sri Lankan army resulting in avoidable loss of life. At the request of President Jayawardane Indian Prime Minister Rajeev Gandhi took initiative to settle the dispute and bring the Tamils into national mainstream. In November 1987 the Parliament adopted legislation establishing the Regional Councils. In the elections that followed Vardaraja Perumal became Prime Minister. However, these efforts failed to satisfy the Tamils and an Indian peacekeeping force was sent to the island to end hostilities and supervise the surrender of arms. However, this also could not achieve the desired result and the Indian peacekeeping force was finally withdrawn in September 1989.

In January 1998 the emergency was lifted and elections were held in February 1998. The United National Party was returned to power. Chandrika Kumaratunga, daughter of S.W.R.D. Bhandaranaike and Sirimao Bhandaranaike became the President of Sri Lanka.

Initially Sri Lanka had a Westminster style Constitution with British monarch as head of state and executive powers, with council of ministers headed by a Prime Minister and a bicameral legislature. In 1972 Sri Lanka became a republic within the Commonwealth. Under the new Constitution adopted in 1978 it now has a presidential system of government with president as head of state, head of government and head of the armed forces with executive powers and a unicameral parliament. The unicameral legislature with 225 members is directly elected for a period of six years by a system of modified proportional representation.

Economy

Agriculture is the mainstay of the economy of Sri Lanka, like other South Asian countries engaging about 45 per cent of the working population. Its predominantly rural population is concentrated in the west, south and southwestern region where rubber, tea and coconut are grown. Paddy remains the principal food crop. Sri Lanka is the third largest producer of tea after India and China.

The main industries are food, beverages, tobacco, textiles, clothing, leather goods, chemicals, petroleum, rubber and plastics. Public sector enterprises accounted for about 60 per cent of the total production. However, it has a dynamic private sector showing good growth despite energy shortage.

With attractive landmarks, such as beaches, waterfalls, thermal springs, wild-life parks, marine sanctuaries, forest reserves, cultural triangle, ancient irrigation works, botanical gardens etc. dotting all over tourism is an important revenue earner for Sri Lanka, though the continuing ethnic conflict has caused considerable damage to its image as a safe tourist destination.

Principal exports are tea, rubber, copra, coconut, textiles, clothing, leather goods and precious and semi-precious stones. Principal imports are petroleum, machinery and equipment, vehicles and transport equipment, food and beverages. Its principal export markets are the USA, the UK, Japan, Germany and Egypt, while its suppliers are Japan, the USA, the UK, India and Saudi Arabia. In 1995 its trade with the SAARC countries stood at US $ 646.7 million, which was about 6 per cent of its total trade and the bulk of it was with India, Pakistan and Maldives. With planning Sri Lanka's economy has responded well and is gradually becoming export oriented.

The banking sector in Sri Lanka consists of 2 large state banks, private, domestic and foreign banks, savings institutions, merchandising banks, venture capital companies, leasing companies and insurance companies. The Central Bank of Sri Lanka is monetary authority of the country.

The package of economic policies introduced by the government in 1977, which provided for stimulation for private sector, attraction for private foreign investment, export oriented activities etc. has been an important factor in its economic growth. Private sector has assumed an active role in most sectors including basic infrastructure such as communication, energy and transport. Inflow of foreign direct investment has risen from Rs. 4,152 million in 1979 to a cumulative investment of Rs. 191,791 million by the end of 1994. No wonder the per capita income of US $ 780 (1996) of Sri Lanka was second highest among the SAARC countries.

Over-all View

The broader view emerging from the country-wise position given above is briefly presented here sector-wise.

Agriculture

Agriculture is mainstay of South Asian economy. It contributed about one-third of Gross Domestic Product (ranging from 24 per cent in Pakistan to 56 per cent in Nepal) supplied roughly one-third of merchandise exports and employed more than three quarters of labour force (ranging from 53 per cent in Sri Lanka to 93 per cent in Nepal).

An important feature of agriculture in South Asia is that in spite of high population growth they have managed to keep the rate of growth of food supply ahead of that of population. However, the distribution of food grains remains inequitable and there has been shortage of pulses and oilseeds.

Agriculture in South Asia is dependent on monsoon that is erratic and varies greatly from year to year. Increase in production, therefore, could be possible through new irrigation systems. About one quarter of India's cropped area is irrigated. In Pakistan the proportion is three quarters, in Sri Lanka a half, in Nepal a fifth and in Bangladesh a sixth. Increase in area under irrigation and improvement in irrigation efficiency hold the key to future growth in agriculture.

Industry and Trade

The development strategies in South Asia have emphasized on industrialisation a great deal. India has a strong base for industrialisation and ranked high among the developing countries. Industrial production has advanced substantially in the region lessening the dependence on developed countries and raising their capacity and strength for participation in international trade. Industrialisation is growing though different countries are at different stage of development. Further the level of technology in use in the region ranges from medieval to most modern and sophisticated.

Foreign trade is important for the economies of South Asia, both as a source of imports and as an outlet for exports. However, their combined share in international trade is still small. It was less than one per cent of total. Imports consist mainly of manufactured consumer goods, inputs for industry and capital goods. Oil is a major item of import.

The main exports were tea, cotton and jute yarn and cloth. The United Kingdom and the United States of America were major trading partners. Gradually a change is taking place in the composition of trade as well as direction of trade. Trade with European and East Asian countries is growing. A shortage of foreign exchange and limited export prospects for a number of primary commodities has limited their participation in international trade. These countries have also suffered due to inflation and worsening of the terms of trade. Bilateral trade relations have been established with some countries. However, the trade among South Asian countries has remained relatively undeveloped. There is substantial scope for the development of this segment for mutual benefit of all the countries.

Tourism

Tourism is emerging as an important economic activity in South Asia. The subcontinent has a rich cultural base, variety in topography, climate, flora and fauna that attract international tourism. Governments in these countries have also promoted tourism by setting up Tourist Guidance Bureaus and providing a variety of incentives for setting up hotels, travel and trekking agencies, training institutes for personnel etc. India, Nepal and Maldives have been the main beneficiary. Most of the tourists come from far off countries, the European countries, the USA, Gulf and Middle East, Japan and East. However, except for between India and Nepal and Sri Lanka and Maldives the internal tourism in South Asia has remained a low-key activity.

Transport and Communication

The travellers in South Asia are frequently struck by the variety of transport in daily life, ranging from porters and pack animals like mules, donkeys and yaks in mountainous region, bullock carts in rural areas to sophisticated rail-road network and airlines in big cities and towns. Over the years the transport system has improved opening up the interior areas, even distant and far-flung places. In India fair weather roads now link more or less all the villages. Its railway network is among the largest in the world. However, because of topography and difficulties of terrain the development has been limited in Nepal, Bhutan and Bangladesh. Inland water transport is also limited except for Maldives and the coastal areas of India. In consideration of limited international trade the sea transport system also has not developed to any significant extent.

The communication system has undergone radical changes since 1980s all over the world and the countries of South Asia have also benefited from it. The post and telegraph system has expanded a great deal. Electronic communication is beginning to make impact. The number of telephones, televisions and radios in use are increasing very fast. Increasingly these systems are penetrating rural areas, empowering people and changing the whole lifestyle. Limited political interaction and lack of inter-country trade have limited the growth of inter-country transport system in South Asia, though transport and communication are identified as important areas of inter-country cooperation in the SAARC.

Energy and Mineral Resources

South Asia is a region of diversity and contrasts, where the nuclear power plants co-exist with cowdung fired household wwens. Most rural housewives, agriculturists, small-scale producers, household and cottage craftsmen still depend upon firewood, charcoal and cowdung for fuel. Bagasse is used for converting sugarcane juice to gur. But at the same time bio-gas generating plants based on animal dung, other non-conventional sources of energy like solar power and wind power are also being gradually adopted in rural areas. Kerosene is replacing the traditional vegetable oils for lighting village homes and shops. Rural electrification is also speeding up the process of change. Electric power is used for lighting lamps, floor mills, irrigation pumps and small-scale industries. Coal and lignite are used in railways, factories and for generating power apart from cooking. The entire road transportation is based on the use of petroleum products. Hydroelectric power is also generated in India, Nepal,

Bhutan, Pakistan and Sri Lanka. Thus gradually the change is coming. South Asian countries have started limited exchange in power resources with Nepal and Bhutan providing hydro-electricity to India and India providing petroleum products to these countries etc. However, it is still limited in volume as well as scope.

With few exceptions mineral deposits in the region are limited to Indian peninsula. India has rich deposits of minerals like iron ore, coal, lignite, lead, zinc, aluminium besides some other small minerals. India is involved in tapping the large deposits of mineral oil. Bangladesh have deposits of natural gas. Pakistan has abundant supplies of limestone and gypsum used in cement industry, dolomite and magnesite used for refractories. Sri Lanka, Maldives, Nepal and Bhutan are not well endowed in this respect.

Finance

South Asia, home of world's largest number of poor, has great potential but to exploit its huge resources are also required at the same time, which it cannot provide. It is a serious policy dilemma faced by the planners. Income levels being low, the capacity to save is also low, though the rate of saving is high. Inflation has been a big destabilisation factor. To supplement the availability of resources from domestic savings attracting foreign capital either as foreign aid from official sources or as loan from private sector at commercial rate of interest have been the alternatives including the World Bank, the International Monetary Fund, the Asian Development Bank and foreign governments. The USA, the UK, France, Germany and Japan have provided funds for various projects in these countries either on bilateral or on multilateral basis. Over the years all these countries have raised funds from these sources.

Whatever their terms, loans have to be repaid, mostly in hard currencies. Debt servicing has become a big drain on the economies of these countries, particularly in the cases of Bangladesh, Pakistan and Sri Lanka. Protectionist policies of the developed countries, rise in oil prices, poor management of national resources, time over runs and cost over runs in projects have further complicated the problem.

Building a financial system responsive to the need of the lenders as well as the borrowers requires substantial improvement in macro-economic management, improvement in the efficiency of the financial institutions and markets and legal and regulatory environment. The world economy is changing very fast and much would depend upon the way these countries rethink their policy options and establish a system which may support development and help these countries in re-aligning their economies *interse* and also with other countries.

An overall view emerging from the description given above is that the countries of South Asia differ considerably in resource endowment and in their economic structures. Thus while India and Pakistan are getting slowly industrialized, Sri Lanka and Bangladesh depend heavily on export of primary goods. Nepal, Bhutan and Maldives are far behind other countries. All these countries pursue inwards looking development strategy and are still pre-occupied with their domestic problems of low national income, poverty, unemployment, illiteracy, poor health standards, etc. Increase in life expectancy has dramatically raised population growth in these countries since the beginning of this century.

Except for India and Pakistan, the economies of all other South Asian countries are small to medium sized. They are unlikely to develop as self-contained economic units. Obviously they have to develop specialized production structure for exports in order to exploit their comparative advantage. This is a legacy of their colonial past. Happily these countries have established trade relations with their neighbours and this is expected to become an effective mechanism for diversification of markets. These countries have adopted medium term planning approach based on the Soviet model of five-year plans.

In recent years there has been consistent good performance in agriculture due to Green Revolution and high yielding varieties. Apart from cash crops such as cotton, jute, sugar cane and tea, these countries have been able to achieve a reasonable level of self-sufficiency in food crop production. Gradually the governments have become aware of the need for greater liberalization in economy by exposing it to world competition, giving larger share to private sector enterprises in trade and industry, simplification of procedures and minimization of physical controls to quicken the process of transition. The basic economic indicators of the SAARC countries are given in Table 2.3.

Table 2.3 : Basic Economic Indicators of SAARC Countries

Country	GDP 1995 in $ billion (PPP)	GDP 1995 per capita $ (PPP)	GNP 1996 per capita income $*	GDP real growth (%)	Composition of GDP in 1995 Agri-culture	Industry	Services@
Bangladesh	145.5	1,130	340	4.6	32.0	17.5	50.5
Bhutan	1.3	730	415	6.0	39.2	30.8	30.0
India	1,408.7	1,500	335	5.5	31.3	27.5	41.1
Maldives	0.39	1,560	900	6.6	31.3	27.5	41.1
Nepal	25.2	1,200	200	2.3	18.7	17.2	64.1
Pakistan	274.2	2,100	465	4.7	40.2	22.0	37.8
Sri Lanka	85.6	3,600	660	5.0	20.0	29.7	50.3

* South Asia Vision and Perspectives, South Asian Region Dialogue, Lahore Independent Planning Commission for Pakistan, 1994.

@ Includes trade, transport, communication, real estate, finance, community social services and other services.

Source : Association of Indian Universities, New Delhi, *University News,* Vol. 36, No. 19, May 11, 1998 , p.18.

It may be observed from the above table that although the countries of South Asia are socially and economically diverse, they have certain common features, like low per capita income, retarded economic growth and industrial exports, dominant position of agriculture in the economy, high degree of government involvement in economic activity through centralized planning, public sector enterprises and govern-mental regulation and control. The World Bank classification puts all these countries in low-income group developing countries.

While the governments in all the countries have shown keen interest in the development of their economies and manpower, the challenge they face is massive. The backlog of major human deprivation in the SAARC countries given in Table 2.4 very clearly shows this.

Table 2.4 : Human Development Balance Sheet of SAARC Countries
(Backlog of Major Human Deprivation in South Asia 1995-2010: in millions)

	India	Pakistan	Bangladesh	Nepal	Sri Lanka	Bhutan	Total (South Asia)
Education:							
Out of School Children : 1995	45	17	9	2.1	0.9	0.2	74
Increase in Primary School-age group (1995-2010)	33	10	7	1.3	0.4	0.1	52
Total Children to be provided Schooling	78	27	16	3.4	1.3	0.3	126
Health:							
No Access to Basic Health care (1995)	140	63	66	n/a	1.3	0.6	271
Additional Population to be proviided Basic Health Care (1995-2010)	286	66	52	9.5	4.3	0.8	419
Total Number of People to be provided Safe Drinking Water (1995-2010)	426	129	118	9.5	5.6	1.4	690
Safe Drinking Water:							
No Access to Safe Drinking Water : (1995)	234	71	26	12	7	n/a	350
Additional Population to be provided Safe Drinking Water (1995-2010)	286	66	52	9.5	4.3	0.8	419
Total Number of People to be provided Safe Drinking Water (1995 –2010)	520	137	78	22	11	0.8	769
Nutrition:							
Number of Malnourished Children (1995)	63	9	13	1.7	0.7	n/a	87
Family Planning :							
Number of Married Couples not Practicing Contraception (1995)	89	3	10	1	2	n/a	105

Table 2.4 (*Contd.*)

	India	Pakistan	Bangladesh	Nepal	Sri Lanka	Bhutan Total	Total (South Asia)
Additional Married Couples (1995-2010)	130	28	18	5	1	n/a	182
Number of Married Couples to be provided Contraception Facilities (1995-2010)	219	31	28	0	3	n/a	287

Source : *Liberal Times:* A forum for Liberal Policy in South Asia, 5(2), 1997 (Published by the Fredrich-Stiftung, Regional Office for South Asia, New Delhi).

Means of transportation and communication are recognized as an essential infrastructure for growth. To an extent they indicate the status of economic growth in a country. The communication profile of the SAARC countries is given in Table 2.5.

Table 2.5 : Communication profile of SAARC Countries

Country	Radio (Per100 persons)	Television (per100 persons)	Newspaper (per 100 persons)	Telephones (per 100 persons)	Post Offices (per 100 persons)
Bangladesh	4	0.5	0.6	0.2	–
Bhutan	2	–	–	0.3	5.5
India	8	3.2	3.2	0.8	17.6
Maldives	12	2.5	1.8	3.7	–
Nepal	3	0.2	0.8	0.3	–
Pakistan	9	1.8	1.5	1	11.5
Sri Lanka	20	3.5	3.2	1	23

Source : Human Development Report, 1994, United Nations Development Programme, pp. 160-161.

It may be seen from the table that except for India and Sri Lanka other countries are still on the lower end. This also brings out that there is an urgent need for greater effort in this direction.

The country-wise description of the politico-social and economic structure of the SAARC countries given above brings out that these countries are still in the stage of transition. The people and the society in South Asian countries have been tradition and culture bound. Democracy has made some difference and now the society is opening up and accepting new ideas. Gradually they are shifting their focus from agriculture to industry and services. Participation of private sector is growing.

Foreign trade is growing. The region is experiencing a rising inflow of foreign direct investment. The economies are slowly moving towards economic integration with rest of the world. Yet a massive dose of development inputs is required to bring up these countries to a stage where they may move with rest of the countries. An idea of the development requirement of these countries can be formed from the estimates of additional cost of essential human investment needed in the SAARC countries, presented in Table 2.6.

Table 2.6 : Additional Cost of Essential Human Investment in SAARC Countries (1995-2010: billion US $)

Objective	India	Pakistan	Bangla-desh	Nepal	Sri Lanka	Bhutan	Maldives	Total (South Asia)
To provide Universal Primary Education to all children	23.0	7.9	4.6	1.0	0.4	0.1	n/a	37.0
To provide Safe Drinking Water to the entire population	24.4	6.6	3.5	1.1	0.6	n/a	n/a	36.2
To provide Access to Basic Health care for the entire population	19.0	6.1	5.8	n/a	0.2	0.1	n/a	31.2
To eliminate Malnutrition among children	0.63	0.09	0.13	0.02	0.001	n/a	n/a	0.9
To provided 80% coverage of Family Planning Services	17.3	3.6	2.4	0.5	0.2	n/a	n/a	24.0
Total	84.3	24.3	16.4	2.6	1.4	0.2	n/a	129.3
GDP (1995-2010)	5878.9	1210.9	626.0	93.9	245.1	5.2	n/a	8059
As % of Cumulative GDP	1.4	2.0	2.6	2.8	0.6	3.8	n/a	1.6

Source : *Liberal Times:* A Forum for Liberal Policy in South Asia, 5(2), 1997. (Published by the Friedrich-Stiftung, Regional Office for South Asia, New Delhi.)

Achievements and Problems of SAARC

During the last two decades while there has been gradual reduction in cold war and relations between big powers have improved, the same is not the case with countries of South Asia. The hangover of the partition of India in 1947 and the Kashmir problem have come in the way of India and Pakistan, the two largest countries in the region, establishing good relations. India and Pakistan had three wars during the last 50 years, in 1948 in Kashmir, in 1965 in Punjab and in Jammu and Kashmir and in 1971 in Punjab, Jammu and Kashmir and in East Pakistan (now Bangladesh). Sri Lanka has suffered heavily due to Tamil militancy and the northern part of the country including Jafna peninsula is still under the control of Tamil Tigers. This gave rise to political uncertainty, diversion of scarce resources from development to purchase of armaments, waging war and conducting anti-insurgency operations.

The countries of South Asia in spite of adverse political relations and other factors have continuously tried to forge close economic and trade links with each other and benefit from such an arrangement. For instance India and Nepal had entered into a Treaty of Trade and Transit for the first time in 1951 under which they provided trade and transit facilities for mutual benefit. The Treaty has been revised and extended from time to time and served the interests of both the countries well. Bhutan and Bangladesh had entered into a trade agreement in 1980 under which each country gave the status of most favoured nation to the other. In 1984 during the visit of King Jigme Singye Wangchuk to Bangladesh the two countries signed one agreement for 'Expansion and Regulation of Trade' and another for 'Economic and Cultural Exchange'. However, while the countries of the region imported items worth 38 billion US $ from other countries, the inter-SAARC country trade was worth 2 billion US $ in 1990, a mere 2.5 per cent of the total trade. Thus, while some SAARC countries exported items like iron ore, steel, rubber, textiles, basic metals, paper, tea, coffee etc. to outside countries some others imported these very items from other countries. The intra-regional trade in South Asia has been at very low level. It was just 3.7 per cent of global trade in 1997-98.

Of late there has been some action in the direction of intra-regional economic cooperation. The South Asian Preferential Trade Arrangement (SAPTA), the South Asian Free Trade Area (SAFTA), SAARC Chamber of Commerce and Industry, South Asian Federation of Accountants (SAFA), SAARC Intellectual Property Forum and Indo-Sri Lanka Free Trade Agreement are some such steps.

South Asian Preferential Trade Arrangement (SAPTA)

At the sixth summit meeting of SAARC at Colombo, the capital of Sri Lanka in 1991, it was resolved to establish a South Asian Preferential Trade Arrangement (SAPTA) by 1997. The Summit declared a "commitment to liberalization of trade in the region through a step by step approach in such a manner that all countries in the region share the benefits of trade expansion equitably." The draft of the SAPTA was approved at the seventh summit meeting at Dhaka in 1993. The objectives have been to open up political and economic frontiers, speed up growth, minimize costs and make efficient use of regional resources to provide wider access to a variety of goods and services at minimum price. This would also boost intra-regional investment and do away with double taxation.

Under SAPTA the member countries have agreed to provide a discriminatory treatment in future. It provides for special and favourable treatment to the least developed countries, namely Bangladesh, Bhutan, Maldives and Nepal, including duty free access, exclusive tariff preferences and removal of tariff and para-tariff barriers. It also provides for technical assistance and cooperation to improve export prospects.

At the first round of negotiations under SAPTA, 226 products were offered for confessional trade. This became operational from December 7, 1995 and onwards. The second round provided concessions for 2000 tariff lines and became operational from March 1, 1997.

Though SAPTA has come into existence its achievements so far are not significant. India has granted 'most favoured nation'

(MFN) status to all the member countries of SAARC including Pakistan, under which it gives maximum tariff concession on trade. The Director General of Foreign Trade (DGFT) of India through their notification dated April 29, 1998 have opened 106 lines for free imports from the six countries of SAARC. This list includes a wide variety of agricultural produce and manufactured items. These items shall have preferential access to the Indian markets compared to other countries. Hopefully, the move will be followed up by substantial duty preferences, as the current duty rate of 45 per cent on most consumer goods is a barrier to trade flows.

SAARC Chamber of Commerce and Industry (SCCI)

The SAARC Chamber of Commerce and Industry, a forum of the captains of trade and industry in the member countries, was set up to promote goodwill and facilitate inter-country trade among the countries of the region. Shri Kanti Kumar R. Podar of India was elected its first President. The objective of the SCCI is to disseminate information and initiate a process of interaction among the business entrepreneurs of the region who are key players in translating the vision of regional cooperation into reality.

For promoting trade and economic cooperation within the region 'trade fairs' are organized by rotation in different countries every year. The first SAARC Trade fair was held at New Delhi in 1997 and the second in Colombo in 1998. The third Trade fair was planned at Islamabad in 1999. For the exchange of online data the SAARC Net, an online computerized data information system, has been set up at FICCINET.

South Asian Free Trade Area (SAFTA)

South Asian Preferential Trade Arrangement (SAPTA), to be established by 2001, was conceived as a transitory phase at the SAARC summit at Male in 1997, to promote greater trade and economic cooperation. The long-term objective was to establish a South Asian Free Trade Area (SAFTA) by 2001 and Economic Union by 2008. At the Male (Maldives) summit of SAARC the target date for the South Asian Free Trade Area was advanced from the original target of 2001 to 2005.

For facilitating gradual movement towards free trade area within SAARC two bodies were constituted, viz., the Inter-Government Expert Group (IGEG) and the Committee of Participants. The Inter-Government Expert Group met at Thimpu and then again at Kathmandu to identify tradable items for the removal of import tariff through product to product approach. The Group has been able to identify 1200 such items. A decision regarding these 1200 tradable items will be taken at the third round of trade negotiations among the SAARC countries. It is proposed to take a sectional and across the board approach for the removal of import tariffs on selected items at these talks. It is also proposed that if the third round of talks succeed, more such items would be identified for free trade among the SAARC countries. The response of Pakistan has been lukewarm to the proposal due to the lack of political will and also the unfounded fear that local trade and industry may suffer rather than benefiting. The report of the International Food Policy Research Institute, Washington D.C. however states that Pakistan (214%) and Bangladesh (194%) would be the major gainers due to food exports. (ET July 29, 1998). However, the progress made so far in this direction is not satisfactory and the Experts Committee has recommended the postponement of the strategy to achieve free trade in the region by 2001.

Another core Group, the Committee of Participants for reviewing the progress made towards establishing the SAFTA, to detect loopholes in the legal framework and give suggestions to plug these deficiencies, is also actively pursuing the task. The SAARC summit in Colombo from July 29-31 1998 had considered the problems and had resolved to work afresh on it.

However, no clear-cut strategy to achieve this objective has been worked out. There are committees but no initiatives. SAARC countries should learn from ASEAN where the ASEAN Free Trade Area (AFTA), set up in 1993 will be a reality by 2003, when the average tariff rates for 38,388 tariff lines in Common Effective Preferential Tariff (CEFT) list would represent 89.1 per cent of the ASEAN tariff lines.

Indian Initiatives

Following the Colombo summit of SAARC, India notified, effective from 1st August 1998, a list of 2400 product groups eligible for lisence free entry from the SAARC countries. This list included consumer goods and durables like colour TV, watches, computers, motor vehicles, plantation products like tea, coffee, pepper, cloves, cardamom, spices and rubber; meat (other than bovine) common salt, liquor, cigarettes; products of leather, paper, textiles, ceramics, glass, metal industry, diamonds and precious stones, subject to goods being new and in prime condition with a minimum 50 per cent material in the FOB value of final product from the SAARC region.

The main beneficiary of the liberalisation in the short run are expected to be Pakistan and Sri Lanka, which have goods to offer. Nepal and Bhutan already enjoy duty free entry. Bangladesh have little exportable surplus. Maldives is a service-oriented economy. However, since Pakistan has not responded positively, Sri Lanka shall be the only beneficiary in immediate future. India wishes to move towards free trade in the region by 2001. This bold unilateral initiative without expecting reciprocity places India in leadership position and is expected to bring rich rewards in future.

India-Sri Lanka Free Trade Agreement

Following the SAARC spirit through a bi-lateral agreement signed in December 1998, India and Sri Lanka have introduced free trade in 600 products. Over the next three years India would reduce duties systematically and would include about 1000 items in free trade list. Sri Lanka has been given 8 years period for this purpose. To prevent misuse of the facility a minimum of 35 per cent value addition within the country has been made essential. This agreement is expected to benefit both the countries, while Sri Lanka would get Indian products at lower price, India would benefit from increased demand of its products.

Indo-Bangladesh Trade

India and Bangladesh have cordial, social and political relationship and are now keen to establish closer trade and economic relationship. Trade and transit are among the priority items on India's economic agenda, whereas Bangladesh wants a bigger market for its goods in India as well as greater investment.

India is seeking transit facility to transport goods to northeastern states through Bangladesh to bring down the cost of transportation and ensure faster movement and use of Chittagong and Mongla ports as transhipment points in return for Bangladesh using Visakhapatnam port for this purpose.

India has offered tea, raw jute, dried fish, jute products, ceramic tableware, insulated cables, leather, glycerin, readymade garments, fruits and agro-products for export. For imports India has already granted special concessions to Bangladesh under SAPTA rules. CII and FICCI have established contacts with their counterparts in Bangladesh and have prepared lists of items India can supply at zero tariffs to Bangladesh. Diplomatic initiatives are also being made to forge trade and economic links.

India has long standing bi-lateral agreements with Nepal and Bhutan, which were revised recently, and greater access has been provided to the products of these countries in Indian market. A beginning has been made in case of Sri Lanka and Bangladesh also, providing concessional rates of duties on goods. There appears to be a beginning of the thaw and this may set a trend for more such initiatives and prepare a ground for SAFTA.

Other Forums of SAARC

Economic cooperation among countries is a highly complex issue and a multi-pronged strategy, rather than a simple and straight approach, alone can succeed. Realizing the complexity in the issues involved other forums of the SAARC have been set up to resolve other pending issues like avoiding double taxation, customs cooperation, transit and transportation facilities, protection of intellectual property etc. among the member countries.

South Asian Federation of Accountants (SAFA)

South Asian Federation of Accountants (SAFA) a federation of the bodies of professional accountants in South Asia was set up in 1984 at the initiative of India. Eight institutes of professional accountants in five member countries of the SAARC are members of SAFA.

SAARC Intellectual Property Forum

To formulate a joint view at the WTO it was resolved to form the SAARC Intellectual Property Forum and an information network on intellectual property at the first consultative committee meeting of SAARC on WTO issues at New Delhi on May 14, 1999. (ET May 15, 1999)

Promotion of Inter-Country Investment

Recognizing the importance of inter-country regional investment and joint ventures in the expansion of regional trade and economic development the SAARC countries have decided to focus more on forging agreements on regional, sub-regional or bilateral basis for the promotion and protection of investment among member states. India had hosted a meeting on 'Promotion and Protection of Investment' in New Delhi during September/October 1997.

Avoidance of double taxation and arrangement for settlement for trade disputes among member states is the other key aspect receiving closer attention.

European Union (EU) a Model for SAARC

European Union is a unique example of sovereign states constructing a supra national institution and alliance, in sharp contrast to Europe's continuing capability of self-destruction through wars, a worst historical legacy. Starting with the European Economic Community (EEC-1957) and the European Free Trade Area (EFTA-1960) as separate blocks, the United Kingdom joined the EEC in 1973, the Community established a

Customs Union in 1967, implemented a Common Market in 1992 and a Monetary Union in 1999. From an unattractive kernel planted into barren ground European Union has grown into a majestic tree spanning half the subcontinent and resting on its own firm foundation.

Key achievements of the European Union over the past three decades have been, creation of a common market for free flow of goods and services from physical barriers, technical barriers, fiscal barriers etc., creation of multi-country infrastructure systems, such as power and gas projects across the countries, rail and road transportation systems, to bring about a fairly uniform level of development among member countries, focusing on initiatives that are of common interest to member countries and which work towards cementing European unity.

The European Union represents a model for third world countries to replicate and build their own organizations, concentrating on economic cooperation, sinking the narrow political rivalries, and increasing political and economic weight. Looking at the background it is observed that the big four of Europe, viz., France, West Germany, Italy and the UK, which largely influenced the European Union, had roughly the same demographic and territorial weight and mutually balanced. This gave confidence to smaller states to join. But in South Asia, India is the sole big power surrounded by smaller states. Under the circumstances it is hardly conceivable that, given the huge difference in demography and economic weight among the states of South Asia, they would be able to form a Customs Union or a Common Market. For the present the target should be Free Trade Area.

Conclusions

Like the European Union and ASEAN, SAARC was formed with high hopes. However, its achievements so far have not been significant. While the member countries have long standing historical, cultural and social links India dominates the economy of the region. India has common border with all these countries. Hence their problems mainly arise from their perception and relationship with India. Some of these countries have long-standing unresolved disputes with India. Other political powers fished in the troubled waters and aggravated the situation to serve their interest. Other member countries do not have the capacity to influence regional power balance significantly. Moreover, these countries faced no threat from any other source. In a way so far the activities of SAARC have really not taken off.

In international politics relations between countries depend upon a number of factors, such as geographical proximity, culture, political, economic and trade relation's etc. National interest of the country, based on economic benefit the relationship is expected to bring, also influenced the relationship. Thus while there has been and remains a vast scope for economic cooperation and trade between the countries of South Asia a bold political initiative to benefit from any such arrangement has been lacking. While the areas of mutual cooperation are well identified they have not been fully explored and exploited.

Trade expansion forms the first stage in economic integration among the SAARC countries. The major constraint in the expansion of intra-regional trade efforts is inadequate recognition of complementarities and economic linkages, which existed for centuries. They need to be rediscovered. Efforts are required for setting up trade facilities, a mechanism as well as a regulated investment regime, realizing the estimated cost of non-cooperation within the region, and a change in the mindset of people and political leadership. All the SAARC countries are in the process of economic liberalization and restructuring, and therefore, keeping in view the ultimate goal of common market strategies should be adopted in harmonization with this larger objective. Side by side necessary concomitants, such as investment promotion, avoidance of double taxation, harmonization in customs procedures and documentation, arbitration and standardization and so on should be explored and pursued. These are the essential elements in transition to free trade area and economic union.

The proceedings at successive meetings of SAARC reveal that South Asian leaders are unable, if not unwilling, to decide the role of SAARC in the rapidly changing international political and economic environment, except for reaffirming the platitudes.

In recent years interest of India in the ASEAN countries has grown. Bangladesh, India, Myanmar, Sri Lanka and Thailand have formed a new association known as BIMSTEC. Efforts for India's entry in ASEAN, Ganga-Mecon Project, bilateral agreements with Myanmar, Philippines, Vietnam and Singapore indicate this shift in India's policy. Some ASEAN countries have also encouraged this for using India against China as power balance.

It is unfortunate that the spirit of mutual cooperation and goodwill has been lacking. The political views are loaded with doubt, fear and distrust. It is, therefore, imperative that the political problems are addressed before any move for worthwhile economic and trade relations. Unfortunately the constitution of SAARC forbids any discussion of political problems at the meetings. But unless these problems are discussed at the highest level they shall never be solved and the SAARC meetings shall continue to end the way they have ended in the past without any achievement.

3

EDUCATION SYSTEM

Introduction

Education is the principal means by which people acquire knowledge, skills and shared values. Individual and ultimately societal ideals and aspirations changes are shaped by education. (Sharma, 1998 p.1)

Education plays a vital role in the process of development. It contributes significantly towards the improvement in the quality of life. This direct link between education and national development can, however, exist only when the national system of education is properly organized. A system of education producing competent professional persons alone can raise the level of productivity and promote economic growth. In this respect the National Policy on Education, 1986 stated that "a human being is a positive asset and a precious national resource, which needs to be cherished, nurtured and developed with tenderness and care coupled with dynamism. The catalytic action of education in this complex and dynamic growth process needs to be planned meticulously and executed with great sensitivity." (NEP, 1986)

Governments have long recognized the importance of primary and secondary education and preventive health care in promoting the welfare of the poor. Not only do improvements in education and health directly affect the well-being of the poor, they also promise greater productivity and wider income opportunities. Countries that have succeeded in providing universal education and reducing infant mortality rates have been shown to have higher economic growth rates. (Vinay Swaroop, 1997)

Education plays a vital role in the process of development and also contributes significantly towards improvement in the quality of life. It may be very emphatically stated that in case of developing countries education and training would yield very broad economic benefits in terms of increased labour productivity, economic growth and reduced fertility rates. There is high positive correlation between women's education and number of children a woman has during her lifetime. In this context it is worthwhile to note that Article 26 of the Universal Declaration of Human Rights proclaimed by the General Assembly of the United Nations in 1948 stated that "everyone has the right to education." The World Conference on Education (1990) had recommended that " education for all by the year 2000 should be the target for the member states." Under the Programme of Education for All by the Year 2000 – the targets to operationalise the programme, stated that "keeping the target of cent-per-cent literacy in view at least 80 per cent of all 14 years old boys and girls should attain a common level of learning achievement, and an access to basic skills and knowledge should be provided for all through adult education." In the light of the above stated objectives let us look at the status of education in South Asian Countries.

Structure of Education

The structure of education in South Asian countries broadly consists of school education comprising of formal school education up to 12th standard and higher education comprising of courses leading to various degrees such as Bachelor degree, Master degree, Master of Philosophy, Doctor of Philosophy, Doctor of Science, Doctor of Literature awarded by the Universities and the professional courses conducted by the universities and professional and other institutions, such as Master of Business Administration (MBA), Master of International Business (MIB), Master of Finance and Control (MFC), Chartered Accountancy (ACA and FCA), Cost and Works Accountancy (CWA), Company Secretaries (CS), Bachelor of Education and Master of Education (B.Ed. and M.Ed.), Bachelor of Medicine and Bachelor of Surgery (M.B.B.S.) and Master of Medicine (M.D.) and Master of Surgery (M.S.), Diploma in Computer Application (D.C.A.) and Master of Computer Application (M.C.A.), Bachelor of Engineering (B.E.) and Master of Engineering (M.E.), Bachelor of Technology (B.Tech.) and Master of Technology (M.Tech.) etc., besides a variety of job oriented certificate and diploma programmes.

Educational Administration

For administrative and operational control of educational institutions a variety of organizational structures have been devised. On the basis of their unique features the educational institutions at work may broadly be either State Funded Institutions or State Funded Special Institutions or State Aided Non-Government Institutions or Un-Aided Non-Government Institutions or Statutory Professional Institutions or Non-Statutory Professional Institutions.

State Funded Institutions

For historical reasons the governments started modern education in South Asian countries. Even today a major share of the cost of education at all levels is borne by the state. All universities and majority of the colleges and schools are funded by the state. Obviously the governments not only have a major say in laying down the policy but also in its implementation.

State Funded Special Institutions

To meet the changing need of education, over the years some special type of institutions have been set up. Maintaining their autonomous character in academic and administrative matters, funds are provided by the governments for special schemes as per their requirement. The national research institutes, the national research laboratories, the IITs, the IIMs in India are such institutions.

State Aided Non-government Institutions

Many philanthropic and religious institutions have over the years come forward and set up educational institutions, colleges as well as schools. Dayanand Anglo Vernacular (DAV) colleges and schools, Sanatan Dharam (SD) colleges and schools, Khalsa Colleges and Schools, colleges and schools run by Christian missionaries in India are some such examples. Recently some trusts, business houses and private bodies have also set up educational institutions. Motivate them to provide mass education and to cover socially and economically deprived sections, keeping down the fee charged, partial state funding is done. Grants-in-aid are provided by the state on meeting certain conditions by the institutions.

Non-aided Non-government Institutions

Some private bodies, particularly those imparting job oriented education, such as management schools and computer education centres, do not depend on state funding. They depend upon their own resources, particularly the fee charged from the students, to meet the cost. Obviously the control of the state in such cases is minimum.

Statutory Professional Institutions

For specialized professional education, statutory institutions have been set up in the countries of South Asia. These bodies are responsible for the regulation and growth of professional education. All India Council of Technical Education, All India Medical Council, National Council for Teacher Education, Institute of Chartered Accountants of India, Institute of Cost & Works Accountants of India are some such institutions in India. Similar institutions have been set up in other South Asian countries also.

Non-statutory Professional Institutions

Wherever the need has been realized, some professional groups have set up their own bodies to regulate the growth of their specialized profession. In fact to begin with most of the statutory professional institutions were set up through private initiative. Later on recognizing their need they were given statutory status.

Public Good, Merit Good or Non-Merit Good

Stage-wise, education is denominated as school education and higher education. The school education consists of primary education (up to standard 5), elementary education (up to standard 8), secondary education (up to standard 10) and senior secondary education (up to standard 12), while higher education consists of general education, technical education and professional education above 10+2 level.

In economic theory the goods and services generated by different institutions and provided to public are broadly classified as public good, merit good and non-merit good. A public good is a good or service where (a) no one can be and need be excluded from enjoying the benefits of the good or service, and (b) any one person's consumption of the good or the service does not affect the consumption of the same by others.

Merit good is a good or service for which the sum of social benefits is greater than the sum of private benefits to the user of the good or service. On the contrary a non-merit good is a good or service where the sum of private benefits to the user of the service are greater than the sum of social benefits.

Applied to education it is observed that primary education up to standard 5, (there is a constitutional obligation under the Directive Principles of State Policy in the Constitution of India, for compulsory education to all children up to 14 years of age under Article 45)* and also elementary education up to standard

---

* "Right to work, to education and to public assistance in certain cases: The state shall, within the limits of its economic capacity and development, make effective provision for securing the right to work, to education and to public assistance in cases of unemployment, old age, sickness and disablement, and in other cases of under served want." Article 41 of the Constitution of India.

"Provision for free and compulsory education for children : The state shall endeavor to provide, within a period of ten years from the commencement of this Constitution, for free and compulsory education for all children until they complete the age of fourteen years." Article 45 of the Constitution of India.

"The Right to Education should be examined for inclusion amongst the fundamental rights guaranteed under the Constitution of India. All the socio-economic measures, without which realization of this right will not be possible, should be taken." - Report of the Committee for Review of National Policy on Education, 1986

8, fall in the definition of merit good. But secondary education up to standard 10, senior secondary education up to standard 12, higher education including technical and professional education cannot be so classified as merit good. However, these at the same time certainly do not fall in the category of non-merit good. The education above the primary and elementary level can certainly be classified as public good as the beneficiary is expected to, apart from limited economic gain for him, benefit the society through the service he shall provide.

However, in case of certain type of technical and professional education, where the basic objective of acquiring the knowledge is to benefit himself only, as the beneficiary trades it for a fee and charges full cost for the service provided, such as advocates and solicitors, consultants, professional accountants, tax consultants etc., these may be classified as non-merit good.

Primary Education

Primary education, which includes the elementary education as well, is the first stage in education. It is the only formal education that children in developing countries, particularly those from rural areas strive to receive. It plays an important role in determining the quality of all subsequent educational attainments by preparing a foundation for the same.

Going into the factors which support the quality of primary education the observation during various studies has been that instructional material, particularly text books, are the most cost effective way of improving the quality of primary education. Guidelines for the teachers and other instructional material designed to assist teachers in organizing classroom activities can also prove cost effective. Strengthening the examination system, mid-day meals and school health programmes, by combating the causes that interfere with a child's ability to learn, also help a great deal.

Secondary Education

With the growth of population and primary education the demand for secondary education has grown all over the region.

However, there is no uniform pattern in all the countries. In view of the resource constraint different countries have drawn alternative strategies. Apart from the normal growth, which can be covered within the budgetary resources, under the strategy of increasing the access and reducing the unit cost per student, increased reliance has been placed on distance education. Further a transition from public schools to private schools has been promoted. Distance education has taken two forms, (a) self-study schools supervised by community members without expensive fully qualified teachers, and (b) extension programmes which typically rely heavily on printed material and do not normally bring students into supervised class-rooms. To promote private schools the management of religious groups, labour organisations and business enterprises have been encouraged to set up schools with fee rates regulated by state authorities. To supplement the above additional provisions for financial assistance and scholarships for the meritorious, the needy and the students belonging to the weaker sections of the society are made.

Vocational Education

Educationists and social reformers have since the beginning emphasized upon making education work based. There have been a variety of experiments in this direction in different countries. For instance, in India Basic Education of Mahatma Gandhi, Buniyadi Taleem of Professor Zakir Hussain, Multi-purpose Schools, Work Experience Programme etc. were taken up during different times with this object. The Kothari Commission (1966) in their report envisaged that the diversification at senior school level should be so planned that about 50 per cent of the students may be attracted to vocational education. The National Policy on Education in India, 1968 also supported the basic philosophy of vocational education by stating that the students should learn to do work, adopt new social values and contribute to the wealth of society.

An important step in this direction was taken by the National Council for Educational Research & Training in India by designing a document titled 'Higher Secondary Education and its

Vocationalisation' in 1976. Vocationalisation was made a separate component at +2 stage. Following the publication of the document areas of vocational education were identified and curriculum were developed to cover these areas. State governments accepted the philosophy and introduced vocational courses, to begin with in large towns and big schools, and at a later stage, gradually to other schools, wherever need was realized or demand was made.

The curriculum for vocational courses was developed through participatory process. The requirement of courses was assessed through the use of new technology, potential available in the environment, aspirations of the society, manpower requirement of different jobs, attitude of the learners, trainers available for different vocations etc. The schools conducting the courses at their level developed some linkage with industries, business enterprises and other institutions for collaborative teaching.

However, it was experienced in India at a later stage that there were difficulties in getting adequate primary data, quantification of future need of manpower, time lag between conducting the survey and institution of the course, lack of inter-district mobility of manpower, state to state differences in developing curriculum and content, lack of pre-service training for vocational teachers, over dependence on the National Council for Educational Research and Training (NCERT) for in-service training of teachers, improper and incomplete managerial organization for policy formulation, lack of inter-agency coordination, certification and accreditation, recognition for jobs, academic and technical support etc.

Vocational education has in a way remained a neglected programme. Though some states in India had set up Vocational Education Councils, there was no national organization for formulating policies and laying down guidelines. Rather the whole organization had been left at the mercy of ill-equipped and apathetic general education system.

Higher Education

Preparing and supporting people in positions of responsibility in government, business and professions is the central and the essential role of higher education. In fact the spread and the quality of higher education largely determine the stage of growth of a country. Universities and colleges are the institutions of higher education. Some autonomous, statutory and non-statutory institutions also function.

Apart from general social objectives, the higher education is intended to "(a) educate highly qualified graduates and responsible citizens able to meet the needs of all sectors of human activity by offering relevant qualification, including professional training, which combine high level knowledge and skills, using courses and content continually tailored to the present and future needs of society; (b) provide opportunities for higher learning and for learning throughout life, giving to learners an optimal range of choices and flexibility of entry and exit points within the system, as well as opportunity for individual development and social mobility in order to educate for citizenship and for active participation in society, with a worldwide vision, for endogenous capacity-building, and for the consolidation of human rights, sustainable development, democracy and peace, in a context of justice, etc." (World Declaration on Higher Education)

Contribution of higher education to development is, however, now being threatened by its three unrelated weaknesses. Firstly, with over-enrolment and less rigorous fields of study the quality of graduates has deteriorated. Second, there is virtual dis-appearance from institutions of higher education of necessary inputs such as repairs, maintenance and replacement of worn out buildings, furniture and equipment, laboratory supplies, multiple copies of text books, journals and monographs in university libraries and committed and service oriented teachers to shape young minds. Third, the cost per unit has become exorbitant while the income inequalities have increased, limiting the students' ability to share the cost. Growing burden on state finances has resulted in large reduction in non-salary recurrent expenditure to below the minimum required level hurting the academic performance.

Country-wise Position

It may be useful here to take an overview of the position of education in different member countries of SAARC.

Bangladesh

Bangladesh had been a part of former undivided Bengal Presidency, which had high traditions of scholarly learning. Dhaka was well known as a seat of learning. However, the situation changed when it became a part of Pakistan in 1947, due to low priority given to education. The level of literacy in Bangladesh also fell very low. As per the 1981 Census literacy was 19.7 per cent in Bangladesh, 25.8 per cent among the males and 13.2 per cent among the females. The compulsory primary education scheme has been replaced by modal primary education scheme. In 1985 there were 42,220 primary schools for 8.920 million pupils, and 9,455 secondary schools for 2.6 million pupils. This increased to 55,280 primary schools for 15.181 million pupils and 11,201 secondary schools for 4,500 million pupils by 1994.

Higher Education

There had been great enthusiasm in eastern part of Bengal for higher education and on the demand of the people a college, Dhaka College, Dhaka was set up in 1841. This was followed by Chittagong College, Chittagong in 1869, Rajshahi College, Rajshahi in 1873, Jagannath College, Dhaka in 1884, Victoria College at Narail in 1886, Brijmohan College at Barisal in 1889, Prabhna Edward College, Prabhna in 1998 and Comilla Victoria College, Comilla in 1899. All these colleges were affiliated to the University of Calcutta, Calcutta till 1947. After independence the affiliation was transferred to Dhaka University, Dhaka.

The first teaching-cum-residential university, the University of Dhaka, Dhaka was set up in Bangladesh (former East Pakistan) in 1921, the only university before independence. After the creation of East Pakistan some more universities were set up, University of Rajshahi in 1953,

Bangladesh (formerly East Pakistan) University of Engineering and Technology at Dhaka in 1961, Bangladesh (formerly East Pakistan) Agriculture University at Dhaka in 1961, University of Chittagong in 1966 and Jahangirnagar University (formerly Jahagirnagar Muslim University), Dhaka in 1970. After the formation of Bangladesh, Islamic University at Tongi in 1986, Shah Jalal University of Science and Technology in 1987 and the University of Khulna were set up. Thus in Bangladesh there were 4 general universities, viz., Dhaka University, Dhaka, Rajshahi University, Rajshahi, Chittagong University, Chittagong and Jahanginagar University, Dhaka, 4 special universities, viz., the University of Engineering and Technology, Dhaka, Agricultural University, Dhaka, the Islamic University at Tongi, the Open University and the University for Graduate Education in Colleges. There are 5 private universities also active in the country.

Higher Education in Bangladesh is imparted in intermediate colleges, degree colleges and university departments. The number of intermediate colleges in 1993 was 384 with 120,694 students and there were 605-degree colleges with 815,701 students besides 10 teachers' training colleges, 49 primary training institutes and 57 vocational institutes. For technical education there are 4 engineering colleges, 2 specialized colleges, 20 polytechnics, 3 institutes, 51 vocational training institutes and 2 technical vocational teachers training institutes. The enrolment in 1993-94 was around 18,500 students. In 1993-94 there were 8,522 students enrolled for MBBS courses, while 337 students were enrolled in 8 post-graduate medical institutions.

The official language in Bangladesh is Bangla (formerly called Bengali), although English is widely used in business and government. English is popular to a significant extent in urban centres and with educated groups. Urdu and Hindi are two minority languages.

Bhutan

Education is still not compulsory in Bhutan. Primary education begins at six years age and lasts for six years. Secondary education begins at 12 years age and lasts for another five years.

Dzonka is the national language of Bhutan. However, English is the language of instructions in schools. Earlier there were no mission schools or private schools. But now the government has granted permission for setting up private schools. In 1994 there were 280 educational institutions with 24,000 teachers and 71,000 students, under the supervision of the Education Division of Ministry of Health and Education. Of these 245 were primary, 28 junior high and high schools and 7 private schools. Education is provided free of charge by the state to its citizens. Bhutan Board of Education conducts the examinations up to 8 class on its own. For class X and class XII the schools have adopted the Indian Council of School Education and Indian School Certificate syllabus respectively. The Council and the Bhutan Board of Education conduct the examinations for these classes jointly. However, it is now being felt that the existing facilities for school education are not sufficient for accommodating all school age children. Many parents, therefore, send their wards for education to India.

However, the overall achievement so far has not been significant. The Human Development Index (HDI) for Bhutan stood at 0.25 in 1992 and the country was ranked 162 among 173 countries in HDI ranking in 1993.

Higher Education

For higher education the Royal Government of Bhutan has set up Sherubtse College at Kanglung, a Royal Institute of Management at Semtokha, Thimpu, Royal Polytechnic Institute at Dewothang, Samdrup Jhonkhar, Royal Technical Institute at Kharbandi, Chhukha and National Resources Training Institute (NRTI) at Lobesa. The Sherubtse College is a multi-faculty fully residential college with faculty strength of 55 and enrolls 500 students. It runs B.Com. (Honors), B.A. (Honors-Economics), B.A. (Honors-English), B.A. (Honors-Geography), BA (Honors-Dzonkha) and B.Sc. courses. The college is affiliated to Delhi University, Delhi that takes care of the academic affairs and also conducts the examinations. English is medium of instructions in all classes in the college.

Some parents send their children for higher education to India. Some slots have been reserved for Bhutanese students in the educational institutions in India under the Colombo Plan. Some students also seek admission under the United Nations Development Programme (UNDP) in Australia, Federal Republic of Germany, New Zealand, Japan, Singapore, the USA, the UK, Thailand, Canada etc. for higher and technical education.

India

India has hoary traditions of scholarly learning. Its scholars created some of the finest literature, much before the dawn of modern civilization. The Takshshila in Northwest Frontier Province and the Nalanda in Bihar were known as great seats of learning, where people from far and wide including China, Tibet, Laos, Cambodia, Burma, East Asia and West Asia came for learning. Bodh Vihars dotting all over the north India were well known as places where the monks provided education in addition to their religious duties. However, during the Moghul period and also the British period the situation changed and there was a great setback in this area.

Independent India started off with the goal of universal literacy. The Constitution of India declared education a responsibility of the state. Article 45 of the Constitution expressed that it will be the responsibility of the government to achieve the target of universal education. Apart from formal education through schools and colleges, therefore, special programmes were formulated from time to time for adult education and spread of literacy among masses. However, over the years this lofty ideal was but progressively scaled down, first to just adult education (for the age group of 15 plus) and thereafter even to young adult (from 15 to 35 years). The successive governments in India have shown awareness of the importance of education in nation building and have provided an increasingly higher allocation for education at all levels, as shown in Table 3.1

Table 3.1 : Plan Expenditure on Different Sectors of Education in India (in Percentage)

Education	First Plan Expdt.	Second Plan Expdt.	Third Plan Expdt.	Plan Holiday Expdt.	Fourth Plan Expdt.	Fifth Plan Expdt.	Sixth Plan Expdt.	Seventh Plan Expdt.		Eighth Plan Outlay
	1951-56	1956-61	1961-66	1966-69	1969-74	1974-79	1980-85	1985-90	1990-92	1992-97
Elementary	56 (85)	35 (95)	34 (201)	24 (75)	30 (239)	35 (317)	33 (836)	37 (2849)	37 (1729)	47 (920)
Secondary	13 (20)	19 (51)	18 (103)	16 (53)	18 (140)	17 (156)	21 (530)	24 (1832)	22 (1053)	18 (3498)
Adult	–	–	–	–	–	–	9 (224)	6 (470)	9 (416)	9 (1848)
Higher	9 (14)	18 (48)	15 (87)	24 (77)	25 (195)	22 (205)	22 (559)	16 (1201)	12 (588)	8 (1516)
Other	9 (14)	10 (30)	12 (73)	11 (37)	14 (106)	14 (106)	4 (108)	3 (198)	2 (118)	4 (751)
Technical	13 (20)	18 (49)	21 (125)	25 (81)	13 (108)	12 (107)	11 (273)	14 (1083)	17 (823)	14 (2786)
Total	100 (153)	100 (273)	100 (589)	100 (323)	100 (786)	100 (912)	100 (2530)	100 (7633)	100 (4727)	100 (19600)

Note : Figures in Parentheses Rs. Crores.
Source : Ayyar, R. V. Vaidhanath, Educational Planning and Administration in India: Retrospect and Prospect, *Journal of Educational Planning and Administration,* Vol. VII, Number 2, NIEPA, New Delhi.

With the efforts made during the past fifty years there have been some achievements in literacy, adult education and higher education. India can be proud of the fact that it has perhaps the largest educational system in the world with about 106 million students at the primary stage, 39 million students at the middle stage, 23 million students at the secondary stage and 5 million students at the tertiary stage of education. (Takwale, 1998, p.3) But over all the entire situation remains dismal. The literacy rate could be increased from 16.6 per cent in 1951 to 36.2 per cent in 1981. With adult illiteracy at 52 per cent, among males at 62 per cent and among females at 35 per cent, the picture looks gloomy. As per an UNICEF study 11 crore children of school going age are out of schools in India, of whom 4 crore were in fact never enrolled.

The Bhartiya Janata Party in their pre-poll commitment (1998) had declared their resolve to make elementary education a fundamental right. The Supreme Court of India have also held that the right to primary education was a fundamental right under Article 21 of the Constitution, which guaranteed right to life and personal liberty, and it was the duty of the state to provide education. Of course, the right to higher education was subject to economic capacity of the state. However, this would require huge resources. Former Finance Minister Dr. Manmohan Singh had estimated the requirement at Rs. 40,000 crore, and looking to the resource position of the government it appears to be a distant dream. A bill introduced in 1996 by Shri S. R. Bommai, the then Education Minister, Government of India, for making elementary education a fundamental right is still pending in the Rajya Sabha.

Higher Education

People in India, particularly those from elite class, have shown great urge for higher education and learning. Many such families used to send their children to England for education, where they made their mark at Oxford, Cambridge and other educational institutions. To satisfy this urge of elite class three universities were set up at the three presidency towns in 1857 on the model of the University of London as affiliating universities, viz., Calcutta University, Calcutta, Bombay University, Bombay and Madras University, Madras. Punjab University, Lahore and Allahabad University, Allahabad were the next to be set up in 1882 and 1887 respectively. Thereafter there was a continuous stream of universities set up one after the other, Banaras Hindu University, Varanasi in 1916, University of Mysore, Mysore in 1916, University of Patna, Patna in 1917, Osmania University, Hyderabad in 1918, Aligarh Muslim University, Aligarh in 1920, Lucknow University, Lucknow in 1921, Dhaka University, Dhaka in 1921, Delhi University, Delhi in 1922, Nagpur University, Nagpur in 1923, Andhra University, Hyderabad in 1926, Agra University, Agra in 1927, Annamalai University, in 1929, University of Travancore (now University of Kerala) in 1937, Utkal University, Bhubaneshwar in 1943, Sagar University, Sagar in 1946 and Rajasthan University, Jaipur in 1947. Thus India had 21 universities at the time of independence. Out of these 19 remained with India and 2 fell in the area of Pakistan, 1 in East Pakistan and 1 in West Pakistan.

After independence, to satisfy the demand from different regions and towns for higher education in different fields including technical, medical, professional etc. more universities, colleges and other institutions were set up.

India has over the years developed a strong base for higher and technical education. Apart from ten central universities, viz., Aligarh Muslim University, Aligarh, Delhi University, Delhi, the Central University, Hyderabad, Indira Gandhi National Open University, New Delhi, Jawaharlal Nehru University, New Delhi, North Eastern Hill University, Shillong, Pondichery University, Pondichery, Assam University, Silchar, University of Nagaland, Kohima, Central Agricultural University, Imphal (Manipur), five Institutes of Technology at Kharagpur, Bombay, Delhi, Kanpur and Madras, five Indian Institutes of Management at Ahmedabad, Banglore, Calcutta, Calicut and Lucknow, five apex agencies for the promotion and coordination of research, the Indian Council of Social Sciences Research, the Indian Council of Philosophical Research, the Indian Council of Historical Research and the Indian Institute of Advanced Studies, in 1994-95 for general education; there were 184 state universities including the deemed to be universities,

886 professional education colleges, and 4862 colleges, with 50 lakh students and 2.8 lakh teachers as shown in Table 3.2.

Table 3.2 : Number of Educational Institutions in India

Category	1950-51	1960-61	1970-71	1980-81	1990-91	1994-95
Schools:						
Primary (000)	210	330	408	495	561	581.3
Secondary (000)	13.6	49.7	90.6	119	151	163.6
Senior Secondary (000)	7.3	17.3	37.1	51.6	79.8	92.252
Colleges:						
General	370	967	2,285	3,421	4,862	6,089
Engineering & Technology	208	852	992	1,317	886	1,230
Medical & Dental	28	60	98	111	128	155
Universities :	27	45	82	110	184*	219*

*Including deemed to be Universities.

Source : India Abstract 1997, Directorate of Audio Visual & Publicity, Government of India, August 1997.

During the post-independence period the number of universities have increased approximately 10-fold, colleges 15-fold and teachers 25-fold. India has over the years developed a very strong base for higher and technical education. This has contributed significantly to the growth of Indian expertise in the fields of Science and Technology, Management, Medicine, Information Technology etc. to world standards.

Hindi, English and 14 other official languages, viz., Bengali, Telugu, Marathi, Tamil, Urdu, Gujarati, Malayalam, Kannada, Oriya, Punjabi, Assamese, Kashmiri, Sindhi and Sanskrit are recognised in India. Hindi is the national language and primary tongue of 30 per cent of the people. English enjoys associate status, but is the most important language for commercial communication.

To sum up education has been recognised as an important aspect of development in India. The government has played an active role in imparting education at various levels, primary, secondary and higher education. The government largely funds technical education, vocational education and university education. Recently private sector has shown some initiative in sharing the responsibility in professional education, particularly in computer education, management education, engineering education, medical education and other types of professional education and vocational training.

However, as indicated by the Human Development Index (HDI), which for the year 1992 stood at 0.38, and the ranking of the country at 135 among 173 countries in 1993, the achievement is far from satisfactory and much more remains to be done in the sector.

Maldives

Formal education is not compulsory up to any level in Maldives. There are three types of institutions for formal education, viz., traditional Koranic schools (Makthabs), Dhivehi-language primary schools (Madarasas) and English language primary schools. Schools of the third category are the only ones equipped to teach a standard curriculum. In 1984 a national curriculum was introduced in these schools.

In 1983 it was estimated that only about 65 per cent of the school age population attended schools. The school enrolment, however, increased by 9.5 per cent between 1984 and 1986. In 1987 the rate of literacy in the islands at 82 per cent was highest in South Asia. It had gone up to 93.2 per cent by 1997. In 1994, the number of schools totalled 264,with 3,855 students enrolled. The coverage of primary schools is nearly complete and significant progress has been made in the coverage of secondary schools, which was 79 per cent of the school going children in 1993. The share of education in budgetary expenditure was 18 per cent in 1993 and education has been the focus area in the investment policy of the government for sustainable equitable growth. This is a creditable achievement for this tiny country consisting of a large number of coral islands.

Dhivehi (Maldivian) is the official language of Maldives. With the development of tourism gradually people are learning English. English is gradually being adopted as business language also.

Higher Education

Though Maldives has made significant progress in school education it has not been possible to establish institutions for higher education within the country. For higher education people in Maldives depend upon India, Sri Lanka, Bangladesh, Pakistan and other developed countries. This has resulted in an over all shortage of professionally qualified and trained manpower who may act as engines of growth in the country. While there is good potential for growth of fisheries and tourism, due to the lack of local entrepreneurship and management skills, it has not been possible to realize the full potential.

Nepal

In Nepal primary education, beginning at the age of six years and lasting for five years, is officially compulsory. It is expected to be provided free of charge in government schools. In 1995 the number of schools at three levels, primary, middle and secondary, was 29,739 with 4.34 million students and 116,258 teachers employed.

Higher Education

For higher and technical education there were three Universities in Nepal. Among these Tribhuvan University was the oldest and the biggest with campuses at Kathmandu and Pokhara. The Purbanchal University has its campus at Biratnagar in southeastern Nepal and the Mahendra Sanskrit University is located at Kathmandu. In 1995-96 a total of 192 campuses were in operation, including 62 campuses of the Tribhuwan University and 130 campuses affiliated to it. Total number of students enrolled in the three universities was 133,680.

Nepal had campuses imparting education in the areas of engineering, agriculture and animal sciences, medicine, forestry and science and technology with enrolment of 17,601 students in 1995-96. The number of students enrolled in areas such as law, management, education, Sanskrit, humanities and social sciences was 75,246.

Tourism has an important place in the economy of Nepal. The Hotel Management and Tourism Training Centre at Kathmandu imparted training in tourism related activities. It imparted training to 716 persons in 1994-95 and a total of 9,479 persons have been imparted training at the Centre till then. Some institutions in private sector were also active in this field.

India due to the long-standing cultural and economic relations with Nepal has made special efforts for providing access to modern education to Nepal youth. For this purpose certain seats have been earmarked for the Nepal students in Indian Universities, Engineering Colleges, Medical Colleges, Agriculture Colleges, etc. Fellowships are provided to Nepal students joining these institutions. Teachers and experts from Indian universities have been deputed from time to time to Nepal under the Colombo Plan to assist educational institutions in Nepal in teaching and research in various specializations. Faculty members from the universities and colleges in Nepal are also encouraged to establish links with Indian universities for research and other manpower development programmes.

Though there have been efforts in this area over the years, however, over all achievement has been low. With the general literacy at 27 per cent the position in fact is dismal. With 86 per cent illiteracy among the females and 59 per cent among the males Nepal is placed at the bottom among the countries of South Asia. The Human Development Index (HDI) for Nepal stood at 0.29 in 1992 and the country was ranked at 149 among 173 countries ranked.

Pakistan

As a part of undivided India before independence the northwest part of India, particularly Punjab and Sindh, were among the economically developed states. During ancient times the great monastery at Takshshila in North West Frontier Province was a well known university from seventh century BC to third century AD, where scholars from all over the north and northwest Asia, Middle East and China came for education. However, due to the successive attackers coming from the west this region remained disturbed and the art, the culture and the education suffered.

Education in Pakistan is still not compulsory, though the country aimed to provide universal primary education for boys by 1983 and for girls by 1987. Primary education begins at five years of age and lasts for five years. Secondary education begins at the age of 10 years and lasts for seven years. In 1986-87 there were 8,081,000 children enrolled at primary schools and 2,661,000 at middle and secondary schools. There were 115,744 primary schools, 10,586 middle schools, 9,657 high schools and 687 secondary vocational schools with enrolment of 11.484 million, 3.472 million, 1.347 million and 0.094 million students respectively in 1995-96 in Pakistan.

The average rate of adult illiteracy declined from 79.3 per cent in 1972 to 73.8 per cent in 1981, 64.0 per cent for males and 84.8 per cent for females. As per the estimates of UNESCO the rate was 70.4 per cent in 1985, 60.1 per cent for males and 81.4 per cent for females. In 1997 also with general literacy rate of 37.8 per cent and adult illiteracy rate of 76 per cent for females and 50 per cent for males Pakistan was placed behind Sri Lanka, Maldives, India, Bhutan and Bangladesh among the SAARC Countries. The Human Development Index (HDI) for Pakistan stood at 0.39 in 1992 and the country was ranked at 132 among 173 countries in 1993.

Higher Education

The history of higher education of modern type in Pakistan starts with the establishment of Government College Lahore, which had a great name in the region. The first university in the region, the University of Punjab, Lahore was set up in 1882, the fourth university in undivided India, after the three universities in the metropolitan towns. However, this was the only university till independence. More universities, colleges and other educational institutions were set up after independence, to satisfy the demand of higher education. Over the years the system has grown and in 1995-96 there were 71 universities, 147 professional colleges and 735 general education (Arts and Science) colleges in Pakistan. The number of scholars on the rolls of these institutions was 24,000; 157,000 and 707,000 respectively.

Urdu is the official language of Pakistan. Punjabi, Pushto, Sindhi and Baluchi are other important regional languages. English is widely used in commerce and industry.

Sri Lanka

The successive governments in Sri Lanka have shown enlightened attitude and realising the importance of education in national development have set up schools and colleges all over the country. Education is officially compulsory for children up to 10 years in Sri Lanka. It is provided free of charge from lower kindergarten to university stage, in state institutions. There are very few private schools. Within South Asia, an overwhelmingly illiterate region, Sri Lanka stands head and shoulders above all other countries. With 90.2 per cent general literacy, 7 per cent illiteracy among males and 13 per cent among females, Sri Lanka is placed at the top among these countries. With high literacy rate it provided educated and trained manpower to foreign investors.

Higher Education

The first institution for higher education to be set up in Sri Lanka was Queens College at Colombo. It was affiliated to Calcutta University in 1859 and prepared students for the public examinations of British universities. The Ceylon University College, Colombo set up in 1921 was the next to be set up. This was raised to the status of University of Ceylon in 1942 with its campus at Paradeniya near Kandy. Vidyadaya University of Ceylon and Vidyalankara University of Ceylon were the next to be set up in 1958. In 1972 the University of Sri Lanka (formerly Ceylon) was broken into six separate universities, viz., University of Colombo, Colombo, University of Jaffna, Jaffna, University of Moratuwa, Katubedde, University of Peradeniya, Peradeniya, University of Kelaniya, Vidyalankara and University of Sri Jayewardenepura, Vidyodaya. The Eastern University of Sri Lanka in 1981, Budhist and Pali University in 1982 and the University of Ruhuwa in 1984 were the next to be set up.

There were 10 universities in Sri Lanka, viz., the Buddhist and Pali University, the University of Sri Lanka, the University of Colombo, Eastern University, University of Jaffna, University of Kelaniya, University of Moratuwa, University of Peradeniya, University of Ruhuwa, University of Jayawardenepura and Open

University of Sri Lanka, which imparted education in areas such as Management, Law, Science, Engineering, Medicine, Dental Surgery, Agriculture, and Veterinary Science. In 1994 the number of university teachers was 2,580 and the number of students was 32,004.

Sinhalese, English and Tamil are the three official languages in Sri Lanka. English is widely spoken and used in business and industry. The total labour force in Sri Lanka was estimated at around 6.1 million with employment rate at 12.7 per cent in 1994. The Human Development Index (HDI) for Sri Lanka at 0.67 in 1992 was the highest among the SAARC countries. It stood 90 among 173 countries ranked for HDI in 1993.

Policy Issues and Problems

The overview of education at school level and higher education level in the SAARC Countries given above, projects a dismal picture. It showed that illiteracy clearly seems to be their dismal forte. Except for Maldives (93.2%) and Sri Lanka (90.2%) the other five member countries of SAARC continue to suffer due to low level of literacy. Among these countries India (52%), Bhutan (42.2%), Bangladesh (38.1%), Pakistan (37.8%) and Nepal (27.8%) are placed among the countries at the lowest level. The rate of adult illiteracy (15 years and above) in the region at 64 per cent for females and 38 per cent for males is higher than world rate of 38 per cent for females and 21 per cent for males, and even higher than the sub-Saharan Africa's 53 per cent for females and 34 per cent for males.

Among these countries Nepal with 88 per cent illiteracy for females and 59 per cent for males presents the worst scenario, followed by Pakistan, 74 per cent for females and 50 per cent for males, Bangladesh, 74 per cent for females and 51 per cent for males, India, 62 per cent for females and 35 per cent for males and Sri Lanka, with 13 per cent for females and 7 per cent for males. This projects the failure of the governments of these countries to achieve the aim of universal primary education and related goals.

Table 3.3 : Literacy in SAARC Countries

Country	General Literacy	Adult Illiteracy(1995)*[2]		Students as (% of Total Population)
		Females (%)	Males (%)	
1. Bangladesh	38.1	74	51	0.37
2. Bhutan	42.2	–	–	–
3. India	52	62	35	0.49
4. Maldives	93.2	–	–	–
5. Nepal	27.5	86	59	0.52
6. Pakistan	37.8	76	50	0.22
7. Sri Lanka	90.2	13	7	0.17
South Asia	–	64	38	–
World	–	38	21	–

* Per cent of those aged 15 years and above.

Source : 1. Association of Indian Universities, New Delhi, '*University News*', Vol. 36, No.19, May 11, 1998, p.18.
2. World Bank Atlas, 1998.

Development Indicators

There has been growing consensus that human development and well-being of people should be measured through selected social indicators. Towards this end the Organisation for Economic Cooperation and Development, the United Nations and the World Bank have identified a core set of indicators, including some in the areas of education and health. (Sanjeev Gupta, 1998 p.12). The United Nations Development Programme (UNDP) publishes a Human Development Report every year which contains a composite index known as Human Development Index (HDI), based on adjusted per capita real GDP combined with educational attainment and life expectancy at birth. It also ranks 173 countries from 1 to 173 on that basis. An abstract of the HDIs for the SAARC countries is given in Table 3.4.

Table 3.4 : Human Development Index for SAARC Countries

Country	Human Development Index for 1992	Ranking among 173 Countries in 1993
Bangladesh	0.309	146
Bhutan	0.25	162
India	0.38	135
Maldives	0.51	–
Nepal	0.29	149
Pakistan	0.39	132
Sri Lanka	0.67	90

Source :Abstract from Human Development Report, 1994 published in the SAARC Chamber of Commerce & Industry, *Study on Opportunities for Intro-Regional Investment Cooperation Amongst SAARC Countries*, Abhinav Publishing Industries Pvt. Ltd., Delhi, 1997.

In fact the root cause of most of the economic and social problems afflicting these countries may be traced to poor quality of education. This also lets out the clue that if these countries are to progress they should make a beginning with their education systems. It may be pertinent to mention here that these countries have a great potential and education is the key to realize this. Over the years these countries have, in spite of all the political, cultural, social and economic problems facing them, made great effort to change and the results may come now.

The world is changing very fast and in the emerging scenario only those institutions and countries may remain afloat which continuously innovate and develop people – creative, efficient, open and committed, who have the abilities to withstand the rigours of sustained hard work.

With a heavy chunk of the public budget as well as private budget spent on education the obvious question is whether the quality of service provided is satisfactory and acceptable and in keeping with the expected standards. While the stagnating enrolment and low quality can ultimately be traced to demographic and economic problems, they are aggravated by inefficient use of available resources as reflected in widespread underutilization of facilities, and a general lack of order and discipline. The infrastructure created for a smaller size is inadequate to meet the requirement of growing numbers.

Strategy for Development of Education

In education, as in any other field, universal policy prescriptions simply do not exist. Based on accumulated evidence over the past fifty years however some broad policy generalizations can be made. For the SAARC countries, which have low per capita income as well as low level of literacy, the best strategy would be to improve the quality and the efficiency of education on the one hand and improve access on the other hand, to provide enhanced learning achievement to the masses entering the stream.

Improving the Quality and Efficiency

Education has an important place among the institutions, which shape and nurture human resource. The quality of the human resource is determined by the quality of education provided. Unless this concern for quality in education is addressed and kept in view through all its stages from entry to exit the effort cannot be considered fruitful.

Administration, Accountability and Governance

The idea of autonomy of educational institutions had its origin in the religious character of early educational system. The education was imparted primarily to ensure that knowledge about theology, divinity worship and the performance of rituals to propitiate the gods and goddesses would pass unaltered from generation to generation and from the priests to the laity. (Anand Sarup, 1994 p.1) Thus for centuries education as a concomitant of religious institutions remained autonomous. However, with the advent of liberalism and rationalism the education system has been forced to change with times. Further during early period education was funded directly by the society. However, gradually more and more of these institutions had to shift their dependence upon governments, private foundations and industry for funding. This brought the question of accountability in the focus.

Autonomy and accountability are the two sides of the same coin. Autonomy without accountability may become dangerous. Accountability is defined as the quality of being accountable or subject to report or justify. Accountability places an obligation upon the agent to provide information of their dealings regarding resources and also subject it to audit by some independent agency or body to which they are accountable. (Sharma, 1999 p. vii) While no institution using public funds can claim absolute autonomy and escape accountability, since educational institutions are required to catalyse the emergence of ideas for a new social order, there is need for insulating them from the rough and tumble of populist pressures and provide them functional autonomy.

As academic institutions become large and more complex, there will be increasing pressure for greater degree of professional administration. At the same time, the traditional forms of academic governance will be under increasing pressure not only because they are unwieldy but also because they are inefficient. The administration of higher education will increasingly become a profession, much as it is in United States. The challenge will be to ensure that the traditional pattern of faculty control of governance and basic academic decisions of the universities' autonomy, academic freedom and commitment to traditional goals are maintained in an increasingly complex and bureaucratic environment. (Altabatch, 1989-90 p.18)

Creation of Knowledge

Two major responsibilities a teacher is expected to shoulder in universities are teaching and contribution to knowledge through research. The purpose of research is to undertake a systematic inquiry into a subject in order to revise facts and theories. Though applied research is carried out in a variety of institutions, such as universities, national laboratories, research departments of government and research installations of industrial enterprises, theoretical research is mainly done in the universities. However, the opinion emerging from the knowledgeable persons does not commend the work being done by some of these institutions. It suffers from a variety of limitations. However, since research has been and remains an increasingly important part of the mission of the academic system in general and universities in particular, it needs urgent attention. In order that the cause does not suffer it is necessary that the universities are provided the necessary facilities on continuing basis. At the same time greater stress should be put on the quality and relevance to the social need in research. For this there should be greater interaction between the researchers and the users of knowledge. (G. Ram Reddy,1980 p.35) Further, the research activity should be integrated with teaching at higher level.

Improving the Access – Supply side Intervention

There are three interest groups having a direct stake in education, the students, the parents and the teachers. For a balanced and healthy growth, therefore, no one group should be allowed to benefit at the cost of the other two. Interest of all the three should receive equal attention. Accepting that education cannot be a profit making activity and the market forces cannot be allowed a free play, the regulatory authority should establish equity and provide justice to all the three. Thus to save teachers from exploitation in a situation of wide gap between the supply and the demand their salary and other claims should be fixed at appropriate level to provide them a decent and congenial life. The fee structure should be kept at a reasonably low level so that students coming even from lower and middle class families may pay and join an educational programme without throwing the budget of their families off balance. At the same time the fee structure should be high enough to provide adequate funds for meeting the legitimate operational and developmental requirements for efficient functioning of the institution. The management's interest in terms of recovering the operating costs as well as the fixed investment should be also provided.

The formal education set up alone cannot be expected to cover all strata and meet the total requirement of the society. The non-formal education should, therefore, supplement on large scale and cover all those strata who need and can benefit from education and just by chance missed it. The system should provide adequate flexibility to cover these groups. Mass awareness should be created and all available resources should be utilized to meet the requirement.

It is realized that the need of education is large and is expected to grow further. However, the quality cannot be allowed to suffer on account of increase in quantity. The attempts for achieving excellence should be pursued in all areas including education and at all levels.

Management of Educational Institutions

The managerial performance in educational institutions leaves great scope for improvement. In this process the students' performance testing system should be made efficient. It should be suitably updated to provide information on learning achievement of the students, quality and performance of the academic and non-academic staff, their training need, options available etc.

Revitalizing the Educational Infrastructure

Revitalization of educational infrastructure to restore quality would involve correction of imbalance between salary and non-salary recurrent expenditure, increased availability of text books and learning material, renewed commitment to academic standards, mainly by strengthening the examination system and maintenance of buildings, furniture, equipment etc. in efficient usable condition, building library and instructional material.

Participation of Public

An inescapable conclusion emerging from the analysis is that the targets of educational programmes cannot be achieved if this remains entirely a state sponsored programme, unless other social groups come forward to participate and share the responsibility and unless some innovative and revolutionary strategies are developed to achieve the goal. It would, therefore, be appropriate for the local community to come forward and assume greater responsibility in the management of educational institutions in their area.

Educated Youth

Young persons have been the biggest beneficiaries of the liberalised education provided by successive governments in South Asian countries during the past fifty years. There is as such an important expectation from them to be fulfilled by helping others to benefit from the educational programmes through motivation, persuasion and incentives, and also by undertaking literacy programmes voluntarily.

Sources of Educational Finance

Diversification in the sources of educational finance is necessary to meet its growing requirement without burdening the state budget. This is possible through increased cost sharing of public education, increased official tolerance of private education and rigorous control of costs.

(i) Rigorous Control of Costs : Most education programmes have suffered due to the lack of resources. In developing countries the demand shall always exceed the availability of resources. Rigorous control should, therefore, be exercised to put the available resources to best possible use. Traditional efficiency measures such as consolidation of dispersed campuses into larger viable units, optimization of the use of existing infrastructure, adoption of technological and management techniques for better management control and efficiency, etc. should be adopted to bring down the unit cost of education.

(ii) Cost Recovery : Under a situation where a disproportionately larger number of students benefiting from higher education including technical education and professional education come from middle and elite group, for the reasons of efficiency and equity, the parents should meet at least a part of the cost of education provided to their wards. In such cases the students may be expected to make better choices, what to study, where to study etc. This would also empower the parents and the students to demand better education for their children.

(iii) Cost Sharing : Except for the universities and state run and state aided institutions the funds for education come from society or parents of the students. In the wake of new economic policy the government is expected to gradually withdraw its financial support from such programmes. Obviously an alternative arrangement has to be made so that education does not suffer on this account. The professional groups, social organizations, public trusts, religious institutions and business enterprises, who are users of educated manpower should come forward and fill the void. The parents should also be prepared to accept increased proportionate burden by paying higher fees.

(iv) Financial Support for Meritorious and Needy Students : With a view to ensuring that the really deserving and meritorious

students do not suffer and are not deprived of education, the financial institutions and banks should provide long term loans on easy terms to students, who may repay the loan along with interest in fixed installments once they get employed.

(v) Involvement of Industry and Private Sector : In the context of increasing access to education to a larger number of students and wide variety of educational programmes, the local community, industry and private educational institutions should come forward to manage the programmes on self-sufficiency basis. There are important implications of these trends. In decisions regarding research and higher education the broader public goals may be ignored. Private interest may not support the traditional functions of universities, including academic freedom, fundamental research and pattern of governance. A usual experience has been that with the emergence of second and successive generations of private management the early munificence and genuine concern for education have waned. (Singh, 1983)

(vi) Vocational Education : Vocationalisation has been emphasized to create technical skills in the work force. While the utility of vocational education is well recognized the way it is organized leaves much scope for improvement. Some recent studies have brought out that many of the students who had studied vocational subjects were found working in jobs unrelated to their training. Considering such evidence coupled with high cost of vocationalisation it is suggested that:

(a) For popularising the programme and greater public acceptability wide publicity should be given emphasizing upon its specific features.
(b) There should be close collaboration between the programme planners, educators, industry and employing agencies in curriculum formulation, organization of instructions and absorption of the product in jobs. National, state and district level councils/committees should be set up for research, development, training and evaluation of the programme.

(c) It is widely believed that vocational competence cannot be acquired unless considerable time is spent for learning the theory and the practice of the vocation. This is possible only through close collaboration between educational institutions and the world of work. The Apprentices Act, 1961 should be suitably amended to cover vocational courses. The students attending vocational course should be taken as apprentice in trade for on the job training and should be paid stipend like other industrial trainees. This will make it easier for the students to get employment after finishing their education.

(d) There should be flexibility about a student joining a course or leaving it at some stage. Thus bridge courses should be developed for those who join in or leave in mid-stream.

(e) Vocational education should also provide for skill up-gradation in case of persons already in service on continuing basis.

Enhancing the Learning Experience

The key to human resource development is not just educating more students but also ensuring that the quality of education is good. In the ultimate analysis the objective of education can be achieved only if there is learning achievement. The teacher-student relationship becomes the most important element in this context. Learning achievement can be possible when the level of interaction and relationship between the teacher and the students and the quality of performance of teachers is good. The actions suggested in this direction are:

Normative Standards

For improving the efficiency of the system the normative standards in terms of expected minimum level of learning achievement for each different level, a normative teacher-pupil ratio, a normative class teacher ratio and a subject teacher ratio should be defined. Likewise the requirement of normal physical infrastructure and teaching-learning material support should be defined.

Teacher Education

Teacher is the most important element in education. For him education is not only a profession but also a mission. Apart from the contractual and professional responsibility he carries as educator in school, college or university, going much beyond it there is an expectation that he would motivate and persuade persons who have somehow remained away from the educational programme, to eradicate the evil of illiteracy. Further he would maintain the highest standards of excellence at work as well as in personal behaviour, as the students learn from him not only inside classroom but also outside it as a role model. It has been shown that devoting more resources to teacher education has the biggest positive impact on schooling. (Vinaya Swaroop, 1997)

To achieve the above objective implementation of teacher qualification standards that extend the length of pre-service general education and increase teachers' knowledge, initiation of the programmes for building teachers' knowledge and skills base through their involvement in research using the most appropriate research pedagogy, organization of continuing education programmes for teachers to equip them with the developments in the area of their specialization, making their career advancement and promotion contingent upon their performance at work, increase the proportion of female teachers and a cross-section of the society among the faculty, arrangement of training for the persons responsible for building, operating and maintaining specific projects for revitalization of education, identification and development of appropriate pedagogy for teaching different courses and subjects and training of the teachers is suggested.

Emphasis on Creativity

True education is expected to liberate the creative spirit of a student, make him think freely and create freely. The formal education system generally lays high emphasis upon conformity and leaves little scope for creativity. Conformity in education can bring out only mediocrity in the end product. Greater emphasis should be laid upon learning through experience to provide stimulus for creative thinking and action.

Creativity is a "man's capacity to produce new ideas, insight, inventions, or artistic objects, which are accepted as being of social, spiritual, aesthetic, scientific or technological value." (Rom Harre and Roger Lamb, 1983)

Applied to education, for creativity teaching should stimulate thinking, feelings and expression, there should be adequate scope for self-expression, and the mental faculties should be developed for independent logical evaluation.

Conclusions

The formal education system in India, which is based on the British system, has over the years become rigid. There has been explosion of knowledge in all disciplines and it is expected to grow further. The need of the society has also changed a great deal in the mean time. Methods and strategies should, therefore, be evolved to meet the changing need of society. The potential and resources of the community should be harnessed to benefit the society at large.

In order that the teachers may adopt creative approach in teaching they should be well informed about the contemporary pedagogic reforms, be trained in the use of innovative teaching methods and the teaching-learning methods used should be continuously upgraded.

Thus, the policy should be to improve the quality by providing critically needed teaching and research material, increase efficiency by reducing unit costs per student and per teacher, introduce self-study method for fees paying part-time students, and encourage establishment of schools and colleges under private management, increasing the rates of fee charged and providing non-instructional services etc.

The general principles stated above can be fine-tuned to the conditions of each country. In South Asian countries primary education should receive higher priority. Details like requirement of infrastructure, teachers etc. should be worked out and considering how much can be provided from what source targets should be set. Once a reasonable level of literacy has been achieved greater emphasis may be given to higher education, vocational and professional education, quality improvement and research.

For long term improvements in education system the governments should develop appropriate policies and mechanism. For implementing the national programme for education, resources required should be mobilised if necessary even with international support and implementation should be done with full vigour and interest. Undoubtedly designing sound programmes to support policy reforms is a difficult process as it entails careful selection, phasing and linking of specific policies from among a wide array of options available for containing costs, diversifying sources of finance and providing necessary services.

An arrangement should, therefore, be also evolved for regional cooperation to learn from each other's experience in the formulation and implementation of educational policies and sharing the experience including sharing the educational training infrastructure. An appropriate forum should be set up under the auspices of SAARC for this purpose.

4

ACCOUNTING EDUCATION

Introduction

Accounting, the art and practice of maintaining records of transactions has undergone complete transformation over the years. It has now come to be recognized as an information support system designed to assist management in carrying out their functions. All organizations, big or small, public or private have accountability to their constituents and accounting properly used, is a powerful tool in creating information to improve the decisions that affect those constituents. (AECC, S-2 June 1992 p.1) It is also being realized now that accounting constituted a multi-disciplinary exercise drawing from economics, law, quantitative techniques, financial management, computers etc. This has necessitated concomitant changes in accounting education also with the object of introducing, equipping and improving the ability of users – students, scholars and practitioners to respond to fast changing economic and non-economic environment.

Accounting Education and Economic Development

Though business education, which includes accounting education also as an important branch of knowledge, has an important role in all economies it is more crucial in case of developing countries striving to make their economies self-reliant and in this process trying to absorb the latest innovations in science and technology for faster growth. There is a constant endeavour in these countries for the development of industries and infrastructure required for development, which requires mobilization of resources from all available sources, and putting the same to optimum use. Development plans are prepared for this purpose and various projects in public sector and in private sector are formulated and implemented. Execution of the development programmes in different sectors of economy is done. The process of planning, programming, implementation and ensuring a wider and fairer distribution of benefits of development requires capable persons with sound knowledge of theory as well as practice of accounting. Without accounting the regime of accountability cannot be established. This signifies the role of accounting and accounting education in economic development. A cursory glance at the history of development in different countries shows that they had more or less similar experience in this respect.

The object of accounting education thus is to nurture and produce accounting academics and accounting professionals and to equip them with theoretical knowledge as well as practical insight in a systematic manner, so that they may take up the challenge of 'accounting' in modern dynamic business environment.

Nature of Accounting Education

Accounting education is essentially multi-disciplinary in nature in the sense that it is greatly influenced by a variety of customs and practices in business world on the one hand and the laws and regulations made by government to regulate business on the other. Accounting practices are not only influenced but are dependent upon a variety of statutory requirements, which include the business laws such as Contract Act, Sale of Goods Act, Transfer of Property Act, Negotiable Instruments Act, Arbitration Act, Partnership Act etc., the corporate laws such as Companies Act, the Monopolies and Restrictive Trade Practices Act, the Foreign Exchange Regulation Act etc., the taxation laws such as Income Tax Act, the Wealth Tax Act, the Gift Tax Act, the Sales Tax Act, the Excise and Customs Duties Act etc., social security laws such as Provident Fund Act, the Public

Pension Act, Payment of Gratuity Act, Payment of Bonus Act, the Minimum Wages Act etc., the industrial laws such as Factory Act, the Workmen's Compensation Act, etc. and the Rules made thereunder.

Accounting education is also influenced by the policy of government, business organizations, accounting bodies and educational institutions regarding accounting practices such as accounting standards, accounting guidelines, audit guidelines, professional code of conduct, system of examinations, training and certification regulation of profession as well as arrangement for education and training of the personnel.

History of Accounting Education in South Asia

Though accounting was recognized as a separate academic discipline at a much later stage its application and use started with the settlement of people in towns and villages and adoption of farming and cottage crafts for livelihood. The need of accounting records was realized by the owners of large tracts of land and business enterprises to create authentic proof of ownership of the land, cultivation, crop income realised etc. With the growth of internal and later on external trade, the system developed into a specialized branch of knowledge. Accountants were appointed by feudal chiefs, traders, indigenous bankers and financiers.

References are available in Indian epics of accounting as a support system for the administration of the state. In Vedic literature the system of land tenure, currency, trade, economic occupations are mentioned at several places. Accountants have been distinctly mentioned in the list of state officials. (Kenneth S. Most, "Accounting by Ancients", *The Accountant*, May 1959, p. 563)

There is a reference in *Valmiki Ramayana* that at the time of Bharat meeting Rama in forest (Bharat Milap) Rama asked Bharat "is your income more than your expenditure and your expenditure less than your income?" (*Valmiki Ramayana,* Ayodhya Kand, Sarg 100) In *Mahabharat* there is a reference of Yudhistir instructing his youngest brother Nakul to look after 'army accounts'. (*Mahabharat,* Shanti Parva, Sarg 40)

However, the history of modern accounting system starts with the efforts made by European traders to open sea routes to different parts of the world after industrial revolution and growth of international trade. It is believed that double entry book keeping originated in Genoa around 1340 A.D. and spread from there to other trading centres like Florence, Milan and Venice in Europe and then to other countries of the world. However, duality the basis of double entry book keeping is also the basis of business transactions, which are based on exchange of goods and services for money or money's worth. Obviously the merchants in all the parts of the world must have had similar conclusions and adopted more or less a similar system for maintaining records of their transactions.

Luca Pacioli, an Italian Pastor born in a small town of central Italy in 1445, who for some time acted as a tutor to the three sons of a rich merchant in Venice, Antonio de Rompiasi, is given the credit for the development of the system. *Pacioli*, after joining the religious order also taught at the University of Perugia from 1475 to 1480 and wrote three works, *The Summa, The Divina and Euclid*. In 1494 *Pacioli* published his *Summa de Arithmetica, Geometrica, Proportionniet Proportionalita*, which was divided into Arithmetic and Algebra their use in trade reckoning, Book keeping, Money and Exchange, Pure and especially applied geometry. Venice granted him ten years copyright on the book. After the expiry of this period the portion of book keeping was published separately in Tuscany under the title *The Perfect School of Merchants*. All this was the outcome of what *Pacioli* learnt and what was being practiced by merchants in Venice over two hundred years.

For organizing the profession the UK gave the lead to other countries and it culminated in the establishment of the Institute of Chartered Accountants of England and Wales in 1880.

In India formal teaching of Accounting along with other Commerce subjects began in 1886, when the trustees of the Pachiyappa's Charities established a Commerce School in Madras. College level education of Commerce including Accounting was introduced in 1913, when the Sydenham College of Commerce and Economics was established in Bombay. Teaching of post-graduate courses in Commerce started in 1921 with the establishment of Commerce Department at Lucknow University. The Post Graduate Department of Commerce was set up at the University of Calcutta, Calcutta in 1922. (Banerjee, 1994 p.56)

Incorporation of Regulation 73 of Table A in the Companies Act, 1888 established accounting as a profession in India. This was based on the Companies Act in Britain. Later on when the Companies Act, 1913 was passed, audit of the accounts of public companies by an auditor holding a certificate from local government (until 1934) and from the Central Government (thereafter until the year 1949) was made compulsory. This created demand for qualified professional accountants. In 1918 the Government of Bombay came forward with a scheme of training of accounting practitioners and professional accountants. The Government Diploma in Accountancy (GDA) was launched and articleship for three years practical training was made compulsory for auditors. The Government of India approved this. Around 1930s the Government of India took over the control of the Diploma for the sake of maintaining uniformity and started conducting a common examination for all the states.

The Government of India also approved the B.Com. Degree of the Sydenham College of Commerce and Economics, Bombay as a qualifying examination, provided accounting and auditing were taken as special subjects. The graduates of the College completing the articleship of three years were declared eligible for the grant of unrestricted certificate of practice throughout British India. (Anil S. Dani, *Chartered Accountant,* September, 1997)

Indian Accountancy Board

Insertion of sub-section 2A to Section 145 of the Companies Act, 1913 in 1930 provided for the framing of rules for issuing certificates and maintaining a register of auditors. In pursuance of the above the Central Government notified the Auditors' Certificate Rules and constituted an Accountancy Board in 1932 by nominating certain representatives of the profession on the Board. The first two Boards were entirely nominated by the Government. The element of election of members to Accountancy Board from among the registered auditors was introduced in 1939. There after the Boards consisted of 12 elected and 7 nominated members. Of the 7 nominated members 3 were government officials, 2 members of the profession and 2 members from trade, industry and commerce. The Commerce Secretary, Government of India used to be the ex-officio chairman of the Board.

The Board advised the Governor General in Council on all administrative matters relating to accountancy, such as maintenance of standards, qualifications and conduct of auditors, granting, renewal and cancellation of certificates of practice etc. However, the final decision in all such matters rested with the Governor General in Council.

Until 1949, Indian accountants were not designated as chartered accountants, since no charter was granted by His Majesty's or Her Majesty's Government. They were known as registered accountants. Among the auditors practicing in India only those belonging to one of the five societies of accountants of the UK were designated as chartered accountants. This established the supremacy of Europeans over the Indians among the accountants and the auditors. In fact a major portion of total audit work remained the monopoly of British audit firms.

Over the years in India thus three categories of professional accountants came into existence, viz., the Registered Accountants (RAs), the Approved Accountants (AAs) and the Holders of Restricted Certificates (HRCs). As on 1st July 1934 the number of the accountants of three categories was 401, 114 and 65 respectively. In July 1940 this number rose to 735, 145 and 54 respectively.

This situation continued till India became independent in 1947. With independence the situation got drastically changed. British India, including Indian states, was divided into two countries, India and Pakistan and later on in 1971 Bangladesh (formerly East Pakistan) became a separate country. After partition each of these countries became an independent country and each one country developed accounting education and accounting profession as per their specific need, though many of the later developments were also similar.

In India on April 19, 1949 the Chartered Accountants Act was passed by the Constitution Assembly of India, it received assent of the Governor General in Council on May 1, 1949 and the Institute of Chartered Accountants of India was set up on 1st June 1949. The Institute of Chartered Accountants of Pakistan was set up on July 1, 1961. Likewise Sri Lanka, Bangladesh and Nepal also had set up the Institutes of Chartered Accountants. The Institute of Cost and Works Accountants of India was set up on 28th May, 1959. Likewise Pakistan and Bangladesh had also set up the Institutes of Cost & Management Accountants in their country to organize professional education and regulate the profession.

At the same time in all the countries of the region the universities and colleges established the departments of commerce or business studies or business administration and initiated the teaching of Commerce. Accounting formed an important subject of study in these courses at under graduate as well as at post-graduate level. Thus the knowledge of theory and practice of accounting became widespread and it became an organized branch of knowledge and also a profession in the region.

Status of Accounting Education

Accounting as a discipline, and also as a profession, has certain unique features. It requires not only sound knowledge base and understanding of the concepts but also their application under variety of situations. This can be possible only through systematic education and training of the practitioners. Though the situation has been different during different times and even today it differs from country to country, the arrangement for education and training of accounting personnel in the countries of Indian subcontinent is broadly as under:

School Level

At school level accounting is taught as a part of Commerce courses at secondary and/or senior secondary level under the academic direction of the concerned Boards of Secondary Education.

University Level

At University level accounting is taught as a part of Commerce and Management courses as a core group of subjects at under-graduate and at post-graduate level under the academic direction of the university board of studies and other academic bodies. However, some national body does the overall coordination and control. For instance in India coordination is done by the Commerce Panel of the University Grants Commission by designing a modal curriculum etc. Support is also provided for the organization of seminars, workshops, extension lectures and refresher courses by universities and colleges.

Accounting group subjects also form part of management education where also the board of studies in management or some other academic body constituted for this purpose formulates the courses. Teaching of these courses is done by the department or the institute as the case may be. The All India Council of Technical Education in case of management courses does regulation, coordination and control.

Professional Accountants

For the education of professional accountants the bodies of accountants or the Councils of the institutions of accountants undertake the responsibility of formulating and approving the curriculum, organizing teaching and conducting examinations for the students enrolling with them for this purpose. This culminates in membership of the Institute in case of those qualifying at the final examinations. The members of the institutes undertake to provide training and work experience to the articles joining with them.

Government Accountants

For the government accountants arrangement for education and training is done by the governments through special training institutions set up for this purpose. In India this is under the over all supervision and direction of the Chief Accounts Officer in

States and the Comptroller and Auditor General of India at national level.

Accounting Education under University System

The university system, which includes the university departments, constituent colleges, affiliated colleges and other institutions of higher education share the major responsibility of accounting education in South Asian countries. Accounting group subjects are taught as a part of Commerce and Management courses.

Commerce Education

Commerce education in the region was started for the first time in India when the Sydenham College of Commerce and Economics was set up at Bombay in 1913. Holders of B.Com. Degree from the college were recognized as professional accountants. Later on it spread to other parts of the country and also to other countries in the region. The existing arrangement in most of the universities has been that while degree teaching is done in colleges, post-graduate courses are conducted by the university departments. Bachelor of Commerce (B.Com), Bachelor of Commerce Honors (B.Com. Honors), Master of Commerce (M.Com.), Master of Philosophy (M.Phil.) are the popular degrees. Accounting forms an essential element in all these degree courses. Specialisation based post-graduate degree in Accounting also awarded by some universities in India and in Bangladesh.

Management Education

Management education is a recent phenomenon in South Asia. However, its growth has been very fast. With the development of trade, commerce and industry, there has been a steady demand for management graduates and most of the students coming out with a management degree are able to find a job. The over all outlook is optimistic and a master's degree in management, whatever the rating of the institution, is a prized possession.

This has attracted the attention of private institutions and most new management institutions are coming up at their initiative. In India there are over 600 institutions imparting management education. There has been an explosion in the number of students joining management courses. The existing business schools in India provide for 40,000 seats. This excludes the open universities (IGNOU and other state universities) which have unlimited reach. Apart from two years regular MBA programme some of the schools run part-time evening programme. Some of the business schools have started specialised correspondence programmes. In Pakistan there are more than 30 business schools, including the Lahore University Department of Management Studies, which has earned global reputation. All the six general universities of Bangladesh impart management education. Sri Lanka has a Post Graduate Institute of Management at the University of Jayewardenepura, set up recently. Nepal has two institutes of management, viz., the Institute of Management at Tribhuwan University, Kirtipur Campus and the University Business School at Kathmandu.

Apart from the IIMs some other business schools also conduct management development programmes for working executives. Among these the Institute of Rural Management, Anand, the National Institute of Bank Management, Pune and the Institute of Chartered Financial Analysts of India, Hyderabad are prominent.

However, all is not well with these institutions. A recent study of the business schools in India by the COSMODE, a research and consultancy group based in Hyderabad, revealed serious quality concerns. Some of their findings are alarming. For instance, although recognized by the All India Council of Technical Education (AICTE), some of these institutes operate from small rented premises; most of the business schools depend upon part-time guest faculty for teaching, while the AICTE guidelines stipulate at least five full time faculties. The curriculum of most of the business schools does not adequately emphasize upon high quality learning and work experience.

The AICTE had sometime back set up a National Accreditation Board to judge the quality of programmes in different business schools. The Board on voluntary basis does accreditation for those coming forward and paying the fee.

Obviously except for some good schools, so far most others have preferred to carry on without rating by the Board.

There is great scope for cooperation in the field of management education among the SAARC countries. Being the largest and comparatively better equipped, India can do a lot to help other countries in this field also, as in many other fields. The Association of Management Development Institutions in South Asia (AMDISA) should initiate action in this direction. It is reported that the Association is planning a South Asian Management Colloquium in Male to discuss issues related with management education. This may bring the desired results.

The knowledge of accounting forms an essential pre-requisite in the training of a modern manager. Obviously accounting education forms an integral part of management courses. The module of accounting subjects in management curriculum generally consisted of financial accounting, cost accounting, management accounting, financial control system, accounting information system, international accounting, taxation, company audit, management audit etc. These subjects are expected to be taught with emphasis on application in business situations, rather than mere understanding of the concepts. With initial clarity of the concepts, there is greater stress on case studies and problem solving approach.

However, under the given regional peculiarities and resource position there is a wide variation in the organizational structure, courses of study, curriculum and method of teaching and examinations.

Country-wise Position

It may be useful here to give the position of Accounting education in countries in South Asia, which are members of SAARC.

Bangladesh

For higher education there are ten universities in Bangladesh, viz., Dhaka University, Chittagong University, Rajshahi University, Jahangirnagar University, Engineering University,

Agriculture University, Islamic University, Science and Technology University, Open University and University for Graduate Education in Colleges. Among these the first four are general universities and impart education in Accounting as a part of Commerce and Business Management courses. Accounting is taught at undergraduate level as a part of B.Com. and B.Com. (Hon.) courses and at post-graduates level as a part of the M.Com. Course. B.Com. is a general two years degree course in Commerce. Students are admitted to the B.Com. Course after ten years of schooling and two years of higher secondary education (I.Com.). B.Com. (Honors) is a three years degree course. Students offering B.Com. (Honors) course on its completion may be allowed directly to offer Master degree in Commerce (M.Com.) course. Otherwise M.Com. is a two years course, where a student is first admitted to one year M.Com. preliminary (Previous) course and on its completion he is admitted to one year M.Com. (Final) course.

There is a separate department of accounting at each of these universities. Faculty positions of Professors, Associate Professors, Assistant Professors and Lecturers are provided as per the requirement of the department for teaching and research activity. In 1986 total faculty positions in these universities were : Professors 324, Associate Professors 588, Assistant Professors 1,222, Lecturers 546 and others 50. The number of scholars on roll was 40,933 with teacher-student ratio at 1:15. This was overall for commerce but all these students also study the accounting subjects.

Accounting is also taught as a part of the Master of Business Management (MBA) course in the first three universities. Dhaka and Rajshahi universities also have a provision for teaching Finance and Marketing in addition to Accounting. Apart from the university departments there are hundreds of colleges under private management and government both, conducting two years degree course in Commerce (B.Com.). B.Com (Honors) and M.Com. (Previous) and M.Com (Final) courses in accounting and management are also conducted in some government colleges.

Bhutan

The accounting education is still in early stage of development in Bhutan. Accounting, Auditing, Cost Accounting, Taxation and allied subjects are taught at Sherubtse College as a part of Bachelor degree course in Commerce. At college level the students are taught as per the Delhi University syllabus, which are based on Indian practices. Bhutan is working towards having the subjects of its own relevance and practices. Some such proposals in this respect have already been submitted to the University of Delhi and some are already through. In the years to come Bhutan plans to have a university of its own with the name Sir Ygyen Wangchuk University. This will provide scope to develop the courses according to the need and the requirement of the country. Some accounting subjects, such as Management Accounting, Financial Management, Management Information System, Management Control System, etc. are also taught as a part of the Post-Graduate Diploma in Financial Management course at the Royal Institute of Management. The Royal Institute of Management (RIM) was established to address the professional need in the area of management. The Institute organizes short-term courses, orientation programmes and workshops in the areas of Accounting, Auditing, Taxation etc. The Royal Institute of Management is also a member of the Association of Management Development Institutes in South Asia (AMDISA).

The above developments are expected to create a suitable ground for the growth of accounting education and accounting profession in Bhutan in the years to come.

Maldives

Maldives, a small country of islands has no arrangement of its own for higher education and also for the education and training of the professional accountants. It entirely depends upon the neighbouring countries, mainly India, Pakistan and Sri Lanka in this respect.

India

A survey of accounting education in India shows that during pre-independence period it mainly implied vocational education. In most of the universities it was taught as a part of Economics or

Commerce. The position, however, started changing around 1950s, with the creation of separate departments of commerce in the universities.

The nomenclature of the faculty of commerce is not the same in all the universities in the country. While in most of the universities it is called the faculty of commerce, some others have a composite faculty of commerce and business administration or commerce and management studies.

Further in most of the universities the administrative department is called the department of commerce, in some others it has different nomenclature. In some of the universities the faculty of commerce has been divided and organized in three or even in four departments. For instance, the M. S. University of Baroda has four different departments under the Faculty of Commerce, viz., Accountancy, Banking and Business Finance, Commerce and Business Administration, and Business Economics. In Rajasthan, the Rajasthan University, Jaipur and the M.D.S. University, Ajmer have three departments each under the faculty of Commerce, viz., Accountancy and Business Statistics, Business Administration and Economic Administration & Financial Management, M. L. Sukhadia University, Udaipur also has three departments under the faculty of Commerce, viz., Accountancy & Statistics, Business Administration and Banking and Business Economics and the J.N.V. University, Jodhpur has four departments under the composite faculty of Commerce and Business Management, viz., Accounting, Business Administration, Business Finance and Business Management. Similar and certain other variations in the organization of the specialization prevail in some other universities also. Commerce faculty thus formed part of the academic disciplines covered in 140 universities out of 226 universities including the deemed universities.

Commerce as a discipline has been popular with students in India and over the years the proportion of students offering commerce courses among the total students has increased from 17.1 per cent in 1975-76 to 21.0 per cent in 1984-85 and to 21.9 per cent in 1995-96 as shown in Table 4.1.

Table 4.1 : Students Enrolled in Higher Education by Faculty - All India

Faculty	1975-76	1984-85	1995-96
Arts	44.5	40.0	40.4
Science	19.1	19.7	19.6
Commerce	**17.1**	**21.0**	**21.9**
Education	3.2	2.4	2.3
Engineering & Technology	4.0	4.5	4.9
Medicine	4.3	3.8	3.4
Agriculture	1.2	1.3	1.1
Veterinary Science	0.3	0.3	0.3
Law	5.8	6.0	5.3
Others	0.5	0.6	0.8
Total	100.0	100.0	100.0

Source : Centre for Professional Development in Higher Education, UGC – Professional Competency in Higher Education, 1996.

The number of students enrolled in Commerce Faculty in the recognised educational institutions in India is given in Table 4.2.

Table 4.2 : Students Enrolled in Commerce Faculty in Recognized Institutions - All India

Year	Number of Students	% Increase (1950-51 = 100)
1950-51	36,347	100
1955-56	58,918	162
1960-61	78,312	215
1965-66	1,57,996	435
1968-69	2,75,385	758
1969-70	3,27,722	902
1970-71	3,54,615	976
1975-76	6,16,983	1,697
1983-84	6,46,654	1,779
1991-92	11,54,804	3,177
1995-96	14,10,119	3,880

Source : For 1950-71: Government of India, Ministry of Planning 1975; For 1975-76, Government of India, Statistical Abstract of India 1982; For 1983-84 Association of Indian Universities, Educational Statistics at a Glance 1987; For 1991-96 University Grants Commission, Annual Report 1995-96.

It may be seen in the above table that the increase in the total number of students offering Commerce in universities and colleges has been phenomenal. The number increased about 38 times during this period, from 0.36 lakh in 1950-51 to 14.10 lakh in 1995-96.

The sex-wise break up of the students in 1980-81 and 1995-96 is given in Table 4.3.

Table 4.3 : Enrolment in Commerce Faculty in India by Stage and Sex

Class	Sex	1980-81		1990-91		1995-96	
M. Com.	Boys	36,464	92.4	47,370	86.7	60,635	76.7
	Girls	3,013	7.6	7,251	13.3	18,377	23.3
Total		39,477	100.0	54,621	100.0	79,012	100.0
B.Com.	Boys	4,13,081	86.0	4,77,367	80.6	7,92,456	76.6
	Girls	67,361	14.0	1,14,666	19.4	3,30,017	29.4
Total		4,80,442	100.0	5,92,033	100.0	11,22,473	100.0
Total	Boys	4,49,545	86.5	5,24,737	81.1	8,53,091	71.0
	Girls	70,374	13.5	1,21,917	18.9	3,48,394	29.0
Grand Total		5,19,919	100.0	6,46,654	100.0	12,01,485	100.0

Source : For 1980-84 Association of Indian Universities, Educational Statistics at a Glance, 1987. For 1995-96 Government of India, M.H.R.D., Selected Educational Statistics, 1995-96.

It may be seen in the above table that over 15 years, from 1980-81 to 1995-96, the proportion of boys had gone down from 86.5 per cent in 1980-81 to 71 per cent in 1995-96, while the proportion of girls had gone up from 13.5 per cent in 1980-81 to 29 per cent in 1995-96. When examined separately for degree and post-graduate courses it is observed that in B.Com. the proportion of boys declined from 92.4 per cent to 76.7 per cent, while the proportion of girls increased significantly from 7.6 per cent to 23.3 per cent during this period. Similarly in M.Com. the proportion of boys declined from 86.5 per cent in 1980-81 to 76.6 per cent in 1995-96, while the proportion of girls increased from 14 per cent to 29.4 per cent during this period.

When the enrolment of students in Commerce stream was examined state-wise as shown in Table 4.4, it was observed that Maharashtra was the leading state. Bengal, Bihar and Gujarat were the other leading states. However, Bihar became the leading state in Commerce education in 1995-96. This was also observed that Commerce has been more popular in large cities and urban areas and also in industrialized states, where the job opportunities for commerce graduates are more as compared to other states (Table 4.5).

Table 4.4 : Enrolment in Commerce Faculty in India by Stage

Stages	1980-81	1983-84	1995-96
M.Com	39,477 (7.6)	54,621 (8.4)	79,012 (6.6)
B.Com	4,80,442 (92.4)	5,92,033 (91.6)	11,22,473 (93.4)
Total	5,19,919	6,46,654	12,01,485

Note : Figures in parentheses represent percentage of total.
Source : For 1980-84 Association of Indian Universities, Education Statistics at a Glance 1987 & For 1995-96 Government of India, M.H.R.D, Selected Educational Statistics 1995-96.

Table 4.5 : Number of Students Enrolled in Commerce Faculty - Statewise

S. No.	State	1970-71	Rank	1995-96	Rank
1.	Andhra Pradesh	24,690	4	95,473	4
2.	Arunachal Pradesh	–	–	225	28
3.	Assam	4,240	13	12,462	16
4.	Bihar	12,545	8	2,55,574	1
5.	Goa	469	19	6,938	17
6.	Gujarat	42,010	3	1,26,450	3
7.	Haryana	1,642	14	15,690	15
8.	Himachal Pradesh	186	21	5,972	18
9.	Jammu & Kashmir	919	18	4,188	19
10.	Karnataka	24,535	5	76,581	5
11.	Kerala	11,794	9	18,086	12
12.	Madhya Pradesh	17,810	6	58,960	8
13.	Maharashtra	87,143	1	2,31,263	2
14.	Manipur	112	23	608	24
15.	Meghalaya	–	–	728	23
16.	Mizoram	–	–	260	26
17.	Nagaland	–	–	367	25
18.	Orrisa	1,160	16	16,404	13
19.	Punjab	1,447	15	16,091	14
20.	Rajasthan	1 4,156	7	18,810	11
21.	Sikkim	–	–	148	30
22.	Tamil Nadu	7,282	11	57,039	9
23.	Tripura	1,152	17	1,926	20
24.	Uttar Pradesh	11,679	10	66,742	7
25.	West Bengal	81,950	2	71,977	6
26.	A & N Islands	–	–	198	29
27.	Chandigarh	419	20	1,615	21
28.	D & N Haveli	–	–	–	–
29.	Daman & Diu	–	–	248	27
30.	Delhi	7,107	12	37,137	10
31.	Lakshadweep	–	–	–	-
32.	Pondicherry	168	22	1,325	22

Source : For 1970-91 Government of India, Statistical Abstract of India 1975. For 1995-96, Government of India, M.H.R.D. Selected Educational Statistics 1995-96.

Courses of Study and Curriculum

After experimenting with different patterns of education, (10) +(2+2), (10+1)+(3), India finally adopted the (10+2)+(3) system in 1986. Under the system after qualifying at the secondary examination (10), a student is required to spend two years in senior secondary class (+2) in school and then enter for the first degree course (+3) of three years in college/university. This is applicable to Commerce courses also. Commerce is one of the specialization areas at senior secondary level under the Central Board of Secondary Education scheme. The state boards have also adopted it. Accounting subjects like financial accounting, company accounts, cost accounting and management accounting form part of it. At first degree level (B.Com.) also accounting subjects like company accounts, cost accounting, management accounting, taxation, auditing, financial control system etc. are taught as a part of commerce courses like B.Com. and B.Com. (Honors). At master degree level (M.Com.) most of the universities provided for a composite package and along with subjects from other areas the students are allowed to offer advanced subjects from Accounting area, such as Advanced Financial Accounting, Advanced Cost Accounting, Tax Planning & Tax Management, Advanced Auditing, Accounting Theory, International Accounting etc. Some of the universities provided for master degree in Accounting, where the students have the option of offering a wide range of accounting courses. Thus depending upon local need, resources and preference the students are allowed to offer accounting subjects at degree and postgraduate level. The situation, however, differed from state to state and also from university to university within the state.

The UGC Curriculum Development Centre in Commerce (1989) did a useful exercise and formulated sets of courses for degree, post-graduation and post-graduate diploma programmes providing adequate flexibility and choice to the students. *(Appendix 4.1)* However, no university adopted these courses as such and the differences have persisted. A similar exercise was undertaken at Mohan Lal Sukhadia University, Udaipur for the universities in Rajasthan. A 'common course' was designed for B.Com. But not much could be achieved since the academic bodies of the universities did not approve the scheme of common course as required under statutes. *(Appendix – 4.B)*

The University Grants Commission (UGC) was established in 1953 by an Act of Parliament to provide funds and to determine and coordinate standards of higher education. However, in view of the diarchy in higher education, with UGC trying to oversee higher education and the state governments regulating it in practice, the UGC has not been able to play its expected role. It has turned out to be a Central Government funds disbursing agency, without powers to enforce its recommendations.

University Grants Commissions have been set in Bangladesh, Pakistan and Sri Lanka also. But it was observed that the role of these bodies in evolving national level curriculum and enforcing academic standards has not been effective.

Nepal

Tribhuwan University, Kirtipur-Kathmandu, Nepal set up in 1961, is the premier university of Nepal having its jurisdiction all over the country. Accounting is taught as a part of commerce and business management courses in the University. The University conducts teaching of Proficiency Certificate in Commerce (I.Com.), B.Com., M.Com. and MBA courses. While the teaching of MBA is done at the Institute of Management in the University campus and the Kathmandu Institute of Management campus, teaching of other courses is done at campuses in Kathmandu, Pokhra, Birganj, Biratnagar etc. B.Com. is a three years degree course and the students qualifying at senior secondary examination (10+2) are admitted to the course. Students qualifying at B.Com. examination are allowed to offer two years M.Com. / MBA course. Some of the colleges also conduct teaching of two years Intermediate Commerce (I.Com.) examination for the students qualifying at secondary examination.

Pakistan

Pakistan has a common history and a common heritage with India and Bangladesh. Till 1947 the three countries were part of

British India. India and Pakistan became independent in 1947 and Bangladesh, which earlier were part of Pakistan, became an independent country in 1971. Obviously the basic structure of education is similar in all the three countries.

For higher education, Pakistan has 71 universities. Important among the general universities are, the University of Peshawar, Peshawar, Gomal University, Dera Ismail Khan [North West Frontier Province (NWFP)], Quaid-i-Azam University, Islamabad, University of Punjab, Lahore, Behind Din Zikeryia University, Multan, Sind University, Jamshoroo, Hyderabad, Baluchistan University, Quetta, Karachi University, Karachi and Azad Jammu Kashmir University, Kotli, Azad Kashmir (established in 1980), Allama Iqbal Open University, Islamabad (established in 1987). Accounting is taught as a part of Commerce and the Business Management courses in all the general universities in Pakistan. There existed either a separate faculty of commerce or a faculty of business management or a department of commerce as a part of the faculty of Social Sciences. The courses offered are I.Com., B.Com., M.Com. and Diploma in Commerce (D.Com.), under the Faculty of Commerce and BBA and MBA under the Faculty of Business Management.

Sri Lanka

In Sri Lanka Commerce and Business Management courses, where Accounting is an important part, are taught at six leading universities, viz., the University of Colombo, University of Jaffna, the University of Kelenia, the University of Peradenia, the Univeristy of Ruhuwa and the University of Jayewardenepura. Accounting subjects form part of the curriculum at under-graduate and post-graduate level both. The faculty of commerce is designated as either the faculty of commerce or the faculty of commerce and business management or as the faculty of business administration.

A review of the Accounting education system in the SAARC countries given above brings out that over the years there has been significant growth in accounting education in these countries. Most of the universities, except for the specialized universities, have arrangement for the teaching of commerce and management courses, where accounting subjects form an essential segment. This has made accounting education mass based and widespread. This also provided a base for professional education.

Major Problem Areas

In spite of all the growth in breadth as well as in depth in Commerce education it cannot be said that all is well. Apart from the general problems of education discussed earlier, Commerce and Accounting education suffered from a variety of unique problems of its own. One major criticism that one hears of Commerce education in general and accounting education in particular is that it does not adequately equip the students for the jobs they are expected to take up later on. Even the students qualifying at the university examinations with high percentage of mark lack in technical and specialized job related knowledge and skills. Their knowledge and understanding of an accountant's work is not up to the mark. They often lack in confidence and cannot take up the work assigned independently.

An inquiry into the causes responsible for poor quality of commerce graduates revealed that apart from the problems afflicting the higher education in general, such as population explosion, resource scarcity, lack of infrastructure etc., over the years commerce education has been developed on the lines of general education, rather than as professional education. The curriculum at under-graduate as well as at post-graduate level have become obsolete, many subjects have lost their relevance, while many pertinent and useful subjects are not being taught. (Manipadma Dutta, 1991 p.76)

The teaching infrastructure, including buildings, furniture, libraries and other equipments and teaching material have not been maintained properly and are in bad shape. There were financial constraints in the way of establishing accounting laboratories. (Sishtla, 1989 p.4)

The number of full-time teachers in general is less than the number required at most of the college as well as universities, leading to greater dependence on part-time teachers and *ad hoc* appointed teachers. This has adversely impacted the quality of teachers. (Banerjee, 1994 p.74) When the teachers are themselves not certain about their own careers how they can concentrate on shaping the careers of their students?

Accountability was lacking in the system and teaching work, the primary work of educational institutions is a neglected activity. The teaching of accounting subjects is loaded with numerical examples of repetitive type. The examinees are in search of five numerical-problems to get a high score. They go for private tuition. Teachers also earn extra tax-free money from tuition. (Khandelwal, 1992 p.53) There is no arrangement for on the job training and the students have no exposure of the world of work. The universities in general were not in a position to provide for practical training in accounting due to the lack of rapport with business and industry. (Sishtla, 1989 p.4)

The existing arrangement for continuing education of the teachers at 'academic staff colleges' and the type of programmes conducted, are not adequate. It does not provide the academic upliftment these programmes are expected to provide.

This brings into sharp focus the need for improving practically every aspect of Commerce education.

Accounting Education in Management Courses

The process of studies in Accounting requires learning through problem solving approach. Solution of numerical problems developed skill required for the solution of real life problems. One has to repeatedly practice this. Since the students joining management courses are drawn from different disciplines, those without Commerce background face difficulty in solving the problems. These students have to devote considerable time to the solution of numerical problems. These students find the subject dry, dull, difficult and monotonous, and as a result they are unable to appreciate the real business situations. (Bhagwati Prased, 1998 p.4)

One of the reasons why management students face this difficulty is that the text books of accounting subjects specially written for management students are not available. The management students study Accounting from text books written for commerce students. Moreover, the teachers of accounting are not trained for teaching management students by case study method. They do not have proper understanding of the requirement of management courses.

It is, therefore, suggested that good quality text books of accounting with management emphasis should be written for these students and the teachers of accounting should be trained to teach management students through case method. (Bhagwati Prasad, 1998 p.5)

Suggestions for Development of Accounting Education

While the role of accounting is well recognized in every organization, the audit work done by professional accountants has been given statutory status in most of the countries, accounting has not been given its rightful status as a separate discipline under the university system in all the SAARC countries.

Nomenclature and Organisation of Academic Bodies

Accounting, a group of core subjects in Commerce and Management education has grown into a complete discipline. It should, therefore, be given the status of a university department focusing on post-graduate teaching and research. (Sharma 1997, p.4) At a later stage the departments may be developed into full-fledged Schools of Accounting, as is the case in the USA. The M. S. University of Baroda (Gujarat) and the universities of Rajasthan in India already have such departments. A specialised post-graduate degree, M.Com Accounting / M.Com. (Accountancy & Statistics) is awarded by these universities. The universities of Bangladesh also have separate departments of Accounting and award master degree in Accounting. On the same line other universities should also set up the departments of Accounting under the faculty of Commerce. The UGC should give recognition to such an arrangement. This would motivate other universities for setting up separate departments of Accounting.

Curriculum Development

Designing a curriculum is a difficult task, as it requires deeper understanding of the societal need in the present and also in future perspective. Availability of resources and efficiency of the system to service the curriculum designed are also important factors in decision making. The universities are the creations of statutes. They are endowed with academic autonomy. The curriculum for different disciplines are designed and approved by academic bodies of the universities through consultations. They reflected the vision of the academy. As the university academic bodies try to guard their autonomy, it is generally difficult to enforce a common curriculum in all the universities. Yet efforts should be made at national or international level with the object of bringing about a reasonable level of uniformity and set appropriate standards.

Curriculum Development Centre in Commerce (1989)

The report of the Curriculum Development Centre (CDC) in Commerce (1989) represented the first effort at national level in India for designing curriculum for different courses in commerce. The report mentioned that commerce discipline has not been properly understood by policy makers in government and also in academy and has been wrongly equated with subjects like Physics, Chemistry, Mathematics or History. This has come in the way of the development of commerce education. After careful consideration of all aspects, the CDC in commerce had divided Commerce discipline into three major areas, viz., Accounting, Business Studies and Business Economics. The CDC in Commerce on that basis developed the entire course structure. (CDC, 1989 p. iv)

The report further suggested that in place of the existing B.Com. Course there should be two major courses at under graduate level, viz., B.Com. (Honors) and B.Com. (Professional). The B. Com. (Professional) course with greater practical input and provision for on the job training was intended to prepare students for different identified jobs/professions spanning the whole spectrum of activities in trade, commerce and industry. B.Com. (Honors) course, with greater emphasis on theory and wider scope for specialization was meant to cater to the need of students going for post graduation. (CDC, 1989 p. v) The curriculum design was kept flexible to provide horizontal and vertical mobility.

For post-graduate level, separate master degree (M.Com.) courses were designed for the three main areas of specialization, i.e., M.Com. Accounting, M.Com. Business Administration and M.Com. Business Economics.

For the students not interested in post-graduate education, keeping the need and expected demand for specialized skills in view, eight different post-graduate diploma courses were suggested. The abstract of the courses suggested for different levels is given in Appendix 4.A.

The Curriculum suggested by the CDC in Commerce for B.Com. provided equal weightage to all the three core areas, and equal number of papers were included from each area. Some new subjects like environmental studies, business mathematics and computer awareness, communication skill were also included. However, the major missing link was subjects dealing with individual and groups behaviour such as Organizational Psychology, Sociology, ethics etc. (Khandelwal, 1992 p.48)

Around the same period the International Federation of Accountants (IFAC, 1986) had suggested curriculum for the education of accounting technicians. The structure of the course suggested was as under:

Preliminary

1. Basic Accounting
2. Communication
3. Business Administration
4. Numeracy and Statistics

Intermediate

1. Accounting
2. Elements of Information System
3. Business Laws
4. Economics and Statistics

Final

1. Financial Accounting
2. Cost Accounting and Budgeting
3. Analysis and Design of Information System
4. Organization and Financial Control
5. Public Sector Accounting and Auditing
6. Public Sector Organization and Financial Control.

Since this was meant for the accounting technicians there was greater emphasis upon applied subjects requiring computational skill and lesser emphasis upon theoretical subjects requiring higher skills. However, this cannot be considered suitable for a general B.Com. or M.Com. Degree, which are expected to have a wider focus.

The recommendations of the CDC in Commerce (1989) and the IFAC (1986) are now more than one decade old. In the mean time lot of changes have taken place in global outlook and the national economies in the region. New challenges and opportunities have emerged. The objectives of university education in accounting should, therefore, be redefined.

In this respect it may be suggested that Accounting education in universities should not merely serve as a feeder for the professional examinations like CA, ICWA etc. It should rather be developed with a wider vision. The development of a discipline can be nurtured only in a truly academic atmosphere and therefore, the university teaching programmes should lay greater emphasis upon concepts, theory building and research, though in a discipline like accounting adequate understanding of practical application is also equally essential. Suitable courses should, therefore, be developed to meet the changing need of business world and also ensure healthy growth of this specialization. The courses developed by the Committee of Courses in Accountancy & Statistics at Mohan Lal Sukhadia University, Udaipur (India) for B.Com., M.Com. and M.Phil. examinations may be suggested as a working model in this respect. The abstract of the curriculum is given as *Appendix 4.B.*

It may be seen that there is balance regarding the number of papers from each of the three specializations at first degree level.

There are two papers from each specialization at I Year, II Year and III Year with provision for option in case of one of the papers at II Year and III Year of B.Com. At post-graduate level each department has a nine papers scheme. All these are specialization papers and provide adequate coverage and exposure of the specialization. There is a separate M.Phil. course for each specialization. This provided for greater emphasis upon the understanding of research methodology, and contemporary issues in specialization.

The UGC Panel in Commerce had organized a two days workshop for the convenors and the heads of the departments of commerce in north zone at Udaipur in May 1999. An intensive exercise was undertaken for evolving curriculum for undergraduate (B.Com.), post-graduate (M.Com.) and post-graduate diploma programmes. The report of the Panel also provided for bachelor and master degrees of the three specialization along with a composite degree. The draft curriculum prepared at the workshop shall be further discussed at the workshops to be organized by the Panel at other regional centres before finalization of the report. It is difficult to say at this stage what shall be the final recommendations. Yet this may be regarded as an important initiative towards evolving a nationally acceptable curriculum of commerce including accounting. However, it may be suggested that along with uniformity adequate flexibility should also be provided in the curriculum, particularly at undergraduate level to take care of regional and sub-regional differences. There should be greater scope for specialization at post-graduate level.

Faculty Development

Teacher is the most important constituent in the scheme of education. The quality of education imparted depends to a large extent on the quality and commitment of the teacher. In an environment that is rapidly changing the teacher is expected to remain tuned to the environmental changes. To an extent due to curriculum changes and peer pressure the teachers may be forced to update their knowledge. But in case of teachers in colleges located at far off places and towns it may not be possible to do so, due to a variety of reasons including non-availability of relevant literature and poor library support.

The University Grants Commission in India had set up Academic Staff Colleges for teacher education. These colleges organise orientation courses for young teachers and subjectwise refresher courses for in-service teachers to upgrade their knowledge. Along with other subjects these colleges organize specialized programmes for the teachers in commerce faculty. It is a common observation that not much has been achieved through this scheme. It may, therefore, be suggested that since the number of university and college teachers is large and increasing, more refresher programmes should be organized and every teacher should be required to attend at least one refresher course every two years, apart from regular participation in seminars, conferences, workshops etc.

As in other disciplines for updating the knowledge of teachers in accounting specialization refresher courses should include contemporary issues in Accounting in the course structure to keep the teachers up-to-date in the subject.

National Eligibility Test (NET)

The University Grants Commission in India conducts a National Eligibility Test (NET) twice a year. A candidate is required to appear at the test in three papers.

Paper I	Objective type general intelligence and aptitude test common for students of all faculties.
Paper II	Objective type test in specialisation paper for the students of a particular discipline. In Commerce this covers various subjects and topics falling in Commerce discipline.
Paper III	Descriptive type specialisation subject question paper.

In Commerce a student has the option to pick one out of six specialisations provided, viz., Accounting and Finance, Taxation, Business Statistics, Auditing and Business Administration.

Qualifying at the NET is considered a necessary condition for the eligibility of a student for Junior Research Fellowship and Lectureship in colleges and universities. Public Service Commissions and State Level Eligibility Test (SLET) Boards in some of the states in India also conduct similar tests. The UGC Fourth Pay Commission (Mehrotra Commission) had recommended that candidates passing the master degree examination with 55 per cent or more marks and also qualifying at the NET should alone be made eligible for Lectureship in university departments and colleges.

While the basic structure of the test is well considered, it is suggested that besides Commerce there should be a full-fledged Paper II of Accounting, covering the subjects like Financial Accounting, Cost Accounting, Management Accounting, Auditing, Taxation and Business Finance for students specialising in Accounting. Further in Paper III the students from Accounting specialization should be allowed to offer Accounting as one of the six specialization subjects given above.

It may be added here that since the teaching of accounting requires in-depth knowledge of accounting theory as well as accounting practice, only teachers with accounting specialization should be selected to teach these papers.

Teaching Methodology and Infrastructure

Teaching of Accounting subjects is different from the teaching of other subjects in commerce and other subjects in social sciences. Accounting courses are highly problem oriented, stress more on computational skill and procedural aspects and less on decision situations. (Sishtla, 1989 p.4) The lecture method used by teachers in theoretical subjects is not suitable for teaching Accounting, as the teacher is required to illustrate the entire exercise visually on the blackboard/screen. To make the teaching of accounting subjects effective it may be suggested that case studies, discussion papers, practice exercises, home assignments etc. should be developed and used for class room teaching. The teachers should further use audio visual aids including computers, overhead projectors, audio and video systems for effective teaching of the subjects.

Rapport with Business

In developing economies closer and continuous rapport between universities and business enterprises is necessary to subserve the human resource requirement of the society. Such rapport should include projection of manpower requirement, identification of changes in the manpower use, development of appropriate curriculum, methods and techniques to meet the changing requirement of education, training and development of manpower etc. The rapport should mean understanding each other's need and helping each other in meeting the same. Such an arrangement already exists in case of professional education of Accounting where the professional accountants provide on the job training to new entrants. A similar arrangement may also be made for university education. Thus the university education programmes should be developed keeping in view the need of business. Business enterprises should share the cost and provide funds for developing teaching material and textbooks, establishing accounting laboratories and also for research. For exposing the young minds to the world of work an arrangement similar to the one made by management schools for their students, should be worked out with business enterprises where by the accounting graduates may be deputed to work with these firms for two to four weeks during summer vacations. These students should be required to present a summer placement report / project report based on the work experience and case study.

Accounting Research

The relationship between quality of research, efficiency at work and quality of output is well recognised. Obviously research is essential in every discipline to widen the horizons of knowledge. This is applicable to accounting also. However, accounting being a practice oriented subject there remains an inherent conflict between teaching and research, while the ideal is combination of teaching and research. As a result research has remained an isolated intellectual activity, and not an essential ingredient of Accounting education.

Research is considered an essential function of universities and as such accounting research is expected to be carried out by faculty members and scholars in university departments. The bodies of professional accountants have also shown some interest in Accounting research. The Institute of Chartered Accountants of India promoted research by offering financial grants for research projects. Some research reports based upon applied research on accounting practices in special situations and fields have also been published in the form of reports, guidelines, monographs bulletins etc. by the Institute. The Institute has also started the publication of a quarterly research journal, 'Management and Accounting Research'. The first issue was published for July-September 1997.

The Institute of Cost & Works Accountants of India have set up a separate Directorate of Research. The Directorate publishes a bi-annual research bulletin. It has also published research-based papers, monographs, guidelines etc. for the benefit of its members. The bodies of professional accountants in other SAARC countries also undertake similar activities.

However, the picture emerging from the description given above is not encouraging. A sample of 326 Ph.D. dissertation taken from 88 leading Indian Universities since 1957 showed that only 39 (12%) of them were in accounting and finance area. (Saeed, 1991) It was also observed that most research problems have remained focused on Financial Accounting, while other fields have remained unexplored.

Researchers often complain about the difficulties faced by them in obtaining information from industry. This reflected a general lack of understanding of the importance of research by business and industry and also lack of coordination between research institutions and industry.

It may be suggested that appropriate areas of research in accounting and finance, which may be expected to contribute to efficiency and quality, should be identified jointly by the researchers and the users of research findings. For instance a very useful research contribution can be made by undertaking research for developing industry norms in respect of capital structure, liquidity, profitability, productivity, input-output etc., for the evaluation of existing practices, identification of regional, national and global trends, verification of effectiveness of the guidelines and standards issued by the SEBI, the ICAI, the RBI, the CBDT and other regulatory authorities etc. Joint efforts by universities, research institutions and business enterprises are needed in this respect.

Indian Accounting Association

The Indian Accounting Association, a body of persons having interest in accounting education and research, has been actively pursuing the cause of accounting education in India over the last three decades.

The body set up in 1968 has an active membership of more than 1000 and 25 branches spread all over the country. Over the years it has organized a number of academic programmes, besides the annual convention at some premier university headquarter in India. Accounting education and research has been a topic of seminar at all national conventions, where members from different part of the country congregated, presented case studies, and research findings and shared experiences on the subject. These ideas are widely disseminated, discussed, modified and adopted by university academic bodies. This takes care of the contemporary issues in accounting education. It has contributed towards better understanding among different national institutions at international forum through the membership of the International Association for Accounting Education and Research (IAAER).

It is a matter of satisfaction that there is wider concern on the issues raised and discussed in this research report. These issues are also being regularly discussed in the academy and also in the profession. The contribution made by the Indian Accounting Association in this area has been significant.

Conclusions

The description given above brings out that there is an urgent need for fresh thinking on the entire arrangement for Accounting education and research under university system in the SAARC countries. In this respect it may be suggested that specialized skill oriented academic programmes should be designed by the universities for the students joining accounting courses. (Sharma, 1997) The Accounting education programmes should be integrated programmes providing for education and training both, so that the students coming out of the universities may find no difficulty in getting suitable jobs and may prove efficient accounting practitioners. For this due care should be taken during the selection of teachers. Proper arrangement should be made for training and knowledge up-gradation of the teachers. Research, the fountain of knowledge, should be given high emphasis it deserves. Research should not be allowed to suffer on account of shortage of funds. Business enterprises should voluntarily cooperate in this endeavour, provide on the job training in their establishments, create endowments and provide financial grants for research.

5

EDUCATION OF PROFESSIONAL ACCOUNTANTS

Introduction

Accountants are the conscience keeper of business entrepreneurs and also the watchdog of society. They have direct responsibility for maintaining the books of accounts, which may reflect the true and fair view of the affairs of business. As professional persons a higher degree of integrity, competence and independence is expected from them. (Sharma, 1997 p.3) Ethical conduct, objectivity, intellectual and scholastic ability, numeric ability, ability to articulate and communicate, ability to analyse and integrate, ability to identify and comprehend business problems, ability to correlate with others and management skill are identified as the essential attributes of a professional accountant. (RCFAE, 1979 p.56)

Historically accounting in India, and in many other Asian countries, had a strong philosophical basis. The 'Niti Sastras' prescribed a comprehensive accounting code. Items of revenue and expenditure were required to be enumerated and clarified giving minutest details. [*Kautilya Arthasastra:* Chapter VII Sloka 23(2)] Sastras also prescribed a strict code of conduct for the persons dealing with public funds, the king and his kins, the ministers, the officers of the state, the accountant and the auditors. [*Shukra Niti:* Chapter VII Sloka 23(3)] The qualifications, powers, duties and functions of all these authorities had been laid down in detailed form as the requirement of their functions. [*Shukra Niti*: Chapter II Sloka 86 and Chapter II Sloka 153; *Kautilya Arthasastra:* Chapter VII

Sloka 23(3) and Sloka 23(2)] Sastras also provided for deterrent punishment to check violation of the code [*Kautilya Arthasastra:* Sloka 23(3)]. Young accountants were expected to be conversant with the philosophy, culture and traditions of the profession. This formed an essential component in their education and training.

Education of Professional Accountant

The accounting profession over the years has grown in so many ways and the status achieved represents an important landmark in its history. The expectations and the demands of the stakeholders are growing. The users of accounting information, such as shareholders, investors, banks, financial institutions, stockbrokers, analysts, government, regulatory authorities depend upon accounting information for information based sound decisions.

The shareholders want to be assured that the company has a reliable and efficient internal control system that eliminates the possibility of mis-statements, errors and frauds. They also want greater disclosure. The managers demand accurate and reliable information on real time basis for efficient operations. The regulatory authorities demand submission of reports and returns in time for monitoring the performance. Thus, the demand for improved corporate governance, better evaluation systems for internal and external performance and increased corporate accountability require accountants to change and raise the quality of the work they perform.

As regards the information available in the annual reports, the educated users say that they provide very little information useful for investment decisions. Users not having adequate background knowledge cannot make out any thing from them. They cannot understand why the assets do not represent their current values and why shareholders' equity has no relationship with market value of the shares. The external users deride the accountants for not disclosing enough, whereas the top management maintains that increased disclosure is not required being costly and likely to harm company's interest. (Bhagwati Prasad, 1998 p.3)

The recent savings and debt debacles, the bank frauds and the stock market scams in India, as in so many other countries, have raised the issue whether accountants and auditors are responsible to the shareholders or the corporate management or the board of directors or the tax paying public or to all of them or none? The accountants' professional standards and code of conduct have of late become a focal point of public discussion.

With globalisation the international trade and services are in the process of evolution. The WTO and the GATS while dealing with the regulatory obstacles to international trade, investment and services take into consideration the status of cross border professional accounting services with the object of ensuring that the foreign service providers, individuals and firms, enjoy the same privileges as their domestic counterparts, there are no discriminatory obstacles and transparency is provided. In relation to the professional accounting services the GATS regulations require that all countries have proper procedures to prescribe, verify and regulate the qualifications for the professionals, the recognition requirements are reasonable and not burdensome and are based on objective and transparent criteria as necessary to ensure the quality of service.

In view of the above the IFAC had recommended that the appraisal process for the professional accountants should be based on the consideration of its three basic components, viz., education, examinations and experience. All these are expected to change in the years to come the entire business environment for the accounting profession.

This brings into sharper focus the need for raising the quality of education, examinations and training of professional accountants, in order that they may meet the expectations of a wider-strata of service users in a wholesome manner. The objective of accounting education and training is to produce such professional accountants and unless the accountants are adequately equipped this objective cannot be realized.

Country-wise Position

In the background of what is stated above a description of the existing arrangement for the education and training of professional accountants in the SAARC countries may be useful here.

Bangladesh

There are two national bodies of professional accountants in Bangladesh, the Institute of Chartered Accountants of Bangladesh and the Institute of Cost and Management Accountants of Bangladesh. Broad details about the two institutes are given here.

The Institute of Chartered Accountants of Bangladesh

The Institute of Chartered Accountants of Bangladesh is the premier body of professional accountants. The central office of the Institute is located at Chartered Accountants Bhaban, 100, Kazi Nazrul Islam Avenue in Dhaka. Md. Anisur Rahman, FCA was President, Mohammad Alamgir, FCA Mohammed Abdul Baree, FCA and Anwaruddin Choudhury, FCA were the three vice-presidents and M.G. Sobhan, FCA was secretary of the Institute in 1999. (SAFA Handbook, 1999 p.1) Detailed information about the Institute may be obtained by visiting the site www.icab.org.

As per the regulations of the Institute of Chartered Accountants of Bangladesh for enrolment as an article trainee, the candidate should hold at least second class bachelor degree (from 1st July 1999 passing the admission test with 60 per cent marks and other examinations with 40 per cent or more marks) and should be more than 18 years in age. Training is imparted for a period of 3 to $3\frac{1}{2}$ years, depending upon the subject studied at graduation, by a practicing chartered accountant who is member of the Institute. The requirement of industrial training is six months. During this period, under the supervision of a chartered accountant in industry, the trainee is exposed to practical accounting and audit work.

The Institute holds examinations for the foundation course (from July 1, 1999), and Professional I, Professional II and Professional III courses twice a year with six month's interval.

There is no restriction regarding the number of attempts allowed. Grades (not marks) are awarded to successful candidates. The Institute provides study material for different papers to candidates registered and appearing at different examinations.

The Institute has two types of members, 'associates' and 'fellows'. A person passing the Professional III examination and completing the prescribed period of training for the articles is eligible to register as associate member. An associate member on completion of 5 years of relevant experience and 60 CPE credit hours becomes eligible for fellow membership. On completion of 2 years continuous membership of the Institute a member becomes eligible for the certificate of practice. The qualifications of certain foreign-chartered accountancy institutes are also accepted for the membership of the Institute.

As on July 1, 1987 there were 516 members of the Institute. Of these 316 were fellow members and 200 associate members. 187 members were doing professional practice and 329 were in service and in other activities. (Table 5.1)

Table 5.1 : Membership of the Institute of Chartered Accountants of Bangladesh as on July 1, 1987

Category of Membership	Fellows	Associates	Total
In Practice	135	52	187
Others	181	148	329
Grand Total	316	200	516

Source : The Institute of Chartered Accountants of Bangladesh, Dhaka.

The Institute of Cost & Management Accountants of Bangladesh

The Institute of Cost and Management Accountants of Bangladesh is the other important body of professional accountants in Bangladesh. The headquarter of the Institute is located at ICMA Bhaban, Nilkhet, Dhaka. Mr. Muzaffar Ahmed, FCMA was President, Md. Abdur Rashid, FCMA and Md. Mujibur Rahaman, FCMA, were the two vice-presidents and Mr. A.B.M. Shamsuddin, FCMA was secretary of the Institute for 1999. (SAFA Handbook, 1999 p.10) More information about the Institute may be obtained by visiting the site www.icmab.org.

The minimum requirement at entry level for the membership of the Institute is graduation level (10+2+2) with 6 points calculated on the basis of academic performance at examinations from SSC (10) to Masters degree. Though there is no training requirement but the minimum time required for passing the whole course is two and a half years. Two examinations are held in a year with a gap of 6 months. There is no limit regarding number of attempts allowed for passing the examination at different stage or as a whole. However, the registration as a student remains valid for 10 years and as such if a candidate fails to pass all the examinations in 10 years time his registration stands cancelled and he may have to seek fresh registration and start again. Exemption is granted to students in certain papers on the basis of equivalence of the level of examination.

For the students preparing for the examinations the Institute conducts coaching through 6 coaching centres located at different places in the country. Such students must attend 75 per cent of the classes held under the coaching scheme to be eligible for examination. Alternatively a student may opt for correspondence course. Students submitting 100 per cent assignments are allowed to appear at the examinations in this case. Study material is provided to such students.

The Institute has two types of members, associates and fellows. A person on attaining 21 years in age, qualifying at the final examination and completing at least 3 years' practical training is allowed to be registered as associate member of the Institute and after 5 years period as associate member and holding higher professional position or in practice with professional exposure is allowed to be registered as a fellow member of the Institute. Certificate of practice is issued after 3 years continuous membership of the Institute. Members of the CIMA (the UK) and the SMA (Canada) are also allowed to become members of the Institute.

Bhutan

Bhutan being a small country has no arrangement of its own for the education and training of professional accountants. It, therefore, entirely depends upon the neighbouring countries, mainly India, in this respect. There is no national body of professional accountants in Bhutan. The professional accountants, who are members of the Institute of Chartered Accountants of India do financial audit, tax consultancy and other related work from India.

India

In India there are two national bodies of professional accountants, the Institute of Chartered Accountants of India and the Institute of Cost & Works Accountants of India. Both the institutes are well established and working for more than fifty years now and contributing significantly to the development of professional accounting education.

The Institute of Chartered Accountants of India

With the growth in the number of professional accountants, the need for an autonomous body to regulate the profession was realized. The Institute of Chartered Accountants of India was set up on 1st July 1949 through an Act of Parliament. Shri G.P. Kapadia was elected the first president of the Institute and served it from 1949 to 1952. The Institute is recognised as a premier body of professional accountants not only in India but also in whole South Asia. The headquarter of the Institute is located at Indraprastha Marg, New Delhi. The supreme authority of the Institute is vested in the Council. Shri S.P. Chhajed was president, Shri G. Sitharaman vice president and Shri Ashok Haldia secretary of the Institute for 1999. (SAFA Handbook, 1999 p.23) Detailed information about the Institute may be obtained from its site www.icai.org.

The Institute had formed five regional councils in 1952, Western India Regional Council (WIRC) at Mumbai (Bombay), Eastern India Regional Council (EIRC) at Kolkata (Calcutta), Southern India Regional Council (SIRC) at Chennai (Madras), Northern India Regional Council (NIRC) at New Delhi and Central India Regional Council (CIRC) at Kanpur. In 1959 it was resolved to set up branches of the regional councils. Across the country the Institute has 81 branches of the regional councils located in important towns of the country.

The Institute normally admits graduates (commerce graduates with 50 per cent or more marks, non-commerce graduates with mathematics with 55 per cent or more marks and other non-commerce graduates with 60 per cent marks) as student trainees. Foreign qualifications recognised as equivalent to bachelor degree of an Indian university by the Association of Indian Universities (AIU) are also considered for registration. The new entrants have to undergo practical training for 3 years if enrolled as article clerk and for 4 years if enrolled as audit clerk (excluding foundation training). The students so admitted are exposed to and get first hand experience of professional accounting work while working with a practicing accountant. The principal is required to give a report on training after the completion of training. There is a provision for industrial training of 6 to 12 months for exposing the students to work in industry, provided the candidate has passed the intermediate examination. The industrial training is done under the supervision of a chartered accountant working in the industry.

The Institute had revamped its education and training scheme with effect from 1st October 2001. Highlights of the scheme are as under :

1. **Professional Course** : The professional course has been divided into two parts, Professional Education (PE)-I and Professional Education (PE)-II.

2. **Eligibility for Registration:**

Professional Education Course I:

- Candidates who have passed the senior secondary examination (10+2) or equivalent recognised examination.
- Graduates/post-graduates who have secured less than specified marks, if Commerce graduates 50 per cent, non-Commerce graduates with Mathematics as one of the subjects 60 per cent and non-commerce graduates with subjects other than Mathematics 55 per cent.
- Provisional registration is available to those who have appeared in 10+2 Examination. Proof of passing the

qualifying examination should be submitted within the prescribed period.

Professional Education Course II:

- Candidates who have passed the Professional Education Examination I.
- Candidates who have passed C.A. Foundation Examination under CA Regulation 1988.
- Candidates who have passed graduation, Commerce graduates with minimum 50 per cent marks, non-Commerce graduates with Mathematics as one of the subject with a minimum 60 per cent marks, non-Commerce graduates with subjects other than mathematics with 55 per cent marks and candidates who have passed the Final Examination conducted by the ICWA/ICSI.
- Provisional registration is available to those (a) who have appeared in PE–I or ICWA/ICSI and (b) Candidates who have passed second year graduation examination and are eligible to appear in the final year graduation examination within six months. Proof of passing the qualifying examination should be submitted within the prescribed period.

3. **Compulsory Computer Training with Hands on Experience** : A student will be required to attend and successfully complete at least 250 hours of computer training with hands on experience as prescribed by the Board of Studies prior to commencement of practical training of three years either along with his Professional Education Course-I or Course-II.
4. **Concentrated Practical Training:** After passing the Professional Education Examination and completing the computer training the candidates will be eligible for admission into the Chartered Accountancy Course, which involves a blend of theoretical education and a practical training of 3 years as an articled clerk with a practising Chartered Accountant.
5. **Restriction on Number of Attempts**: A student will have to pass PE-I and PE-II within five consecutive attempts. For the purpose of reckoning the maximum permissible number of

five attempts, only those examinations which follow the issue of eligibility certificates by satisfying the requirements of the scheme will be taken in to account. Non-appearance in an eligible attempt will also be reckoned as an attempt for this purpose.

6. **Compulsory Course on General Management and Communication Skill :** An article clerk who has completed the practical training and passed the Final examination as per the new syllabus is required to attend a Programme on General Management and Communication Skills or such other programme as prescribed by the Council from time to time, before applying for membership of Institute.
7. Final Examination during last six months of training or there-after.
8. Cut-off Dates for Registration for PE-I and PE-II for May examination is 30th June of the preceding year and for November examination is 31st December of the preceding year.

Theoretical knowledge is provided through postal coaching, revisionary classes, Sunday tests and oral coaching classes at selected centres in the country. All students within the city jurisdiction of Ahmedabad, Jaipur, Kanpur, Calcutta, Coimbatore, Delhi, Hyderabad, Madras and Poona are governed by the Sunday test scheme and the students qualifying in requisite number of test papers are given eligibility for appearing at the Intermediate examination. At other places the students have to obtain their eligibility by submitting the assignments and clearing the test papers under postal coaching scheme. Accreditation has been given to some selected institutions for oral coaching of the students for Intermediate examination papers.

The Institute introduced Foundation Course in April 1992, as a pre-professional teaching course, with the object of attracting young students having aptitude for accounting and audit work. It had given accreditation to 125 institutions affiliated to various universities in India for conducting oral coaching classes for these students, in addition to its arrangement for postal coaching through the regional centres.

The Examination Directorate of the Institute conducts examinations of CA Foundation, Intermediate and Final and post-graduate Course in Management Accountancy etc. at different centres in May and November every year. There is no grading system and marks are awarded at the examinations. A student securing 40 per cent or more marks in individual papers and 50 per cent or more marks in the aggregate is declared as pass. In 1985 an examination centre was opened at Dubai and in 1987 at Kathmandu.

The growth in enrolment of students is shown in Table 5.2. It may be seen that enrolment of students has grown from 257 in 1949 to 1,961 in 1954-55 and to 21,354 in 1996-97.

Table 5.2 : Enrolment of Students by ICAI, New Delhi

Year	No. of Students Enrolled	Increase/Decrease in Enrolment
1949	257	-
1954-55	1,961	1,704
1965-66	2,822	861
1969-70	2,915	93
1974-75	3,464	549
1979-80	10,133	6,669
1983-84	8,660	(-)1,473
1986-87	10,642	1,982
1987-88	12,753	2,111
1988-89	13,990	1,237
1989-90	13,305	(-) 685
1990-91	12,791	514
1996-97	21,354	8,563

Source : The Institute of Chartered Accountants of India, New Delhi.

The Technical Directorate and the regional councils of the Institute conduct continuing education programmes and post-qualification courses, such as Management Accountancy, Corporate Management and Tax Management.

For liaison with the universities, colleges, boards of secondary education and senior secondary schools, the Institute had set up a Liaison Committee in 1969. The Committee maintains liaison by floating model syllabus for B.Com., coordination in teaching of CA Courses, supporting research, holding joint seminars on topics of mutual interest etc.

The Institute is member of the International Accounting Standards Committee since 1974. The responsibility of formulation of Indian Accounting Standards has been undertaken by the Accounting Standards Board, which works under the Institute. Since its establishment in 1975 the Board has formulated 15 Accounting Standards by 1999. In 1990 the process of mandating the Accounting Standards was started and 13 Accounting Standards are mandatory and 2 are recommendatory. The Auditing Practices Committee of the Institute prepares and issues Standard Auditing Practices and guidance notes for the benefit and use by the practitioners, students and scholars.

The Institute offers two types of membership, associate membership and fellow membership. A person 21 years or more in age on passing the CA final examination and completing the practical training becomes eligible for associate membership. An associate member with five years continuous associate membership and 5 years practice as chartered accountant or 5 years employment in an industrial/commercial undertaking becomes eligible for fellow membership. Members not involved in any other business are considered eligible for the certificate of practice. No other examinations are considered as equivalent to the CA examinations. Persons qualifying at the examination of the chartered accountants institute of England were allowed to be registered as members till December 8, 1995. Now this facility does not exists. The membership of the Institute was 82,500 in March 1998. At the present rate of growth it is estimated to become 140,000 by 2025 and 190,000 by 2050. The growth of membership of the Institute since its inception is given in Table 5.3. It may be seen from the table that the membership of the Institute has steadily grown over the years at the rate of 6 to 8 per cent per year.

As on 1st April 1991, out of 58,998 members of the Institute, 22,136 (37%) were fellow members and 36,862 (63%) were associate members. Of the above members, 35,364 (59%) were in full-time practice, 8,062 (13%) in part-time practice and the rest 15,762 (26%) were not in practice. (Table 5.4)

Table 5.3 : Membership of the Institute of Chartered Accountants of India

Year	Number of Members		
	Enrolment	Membership	Growth
July 1949	1,685	1,685	—
March 1951	263	1,948	15.95
March 1956	1,431	3,379	11.64
March 1958	786	4,165	23.26
March 1961	777	4,942	7.90
March 1966	2,390	7,332	8.20
March 1971	3,895	11,227	8.89
March 1976	5,538	16,765	
March 1981	8,675	25,438	8.69
March 1986	14,840	40,278	9.62
March 1987	4,356	44,634	8.89
March 1988	4,690	49,324	8.34
March 1989	3,810	53,134	8.69
March 1990	3,439	56,573	9.62
March 1991	2,425	58,998	7.93
March 1994	9,463	68,461	5.08
March 1995	2,502	70,963	3.65
March 1996	3,399	74,362	4.70
March 1997	4,144	78,506	5.50
March 1998	4,006	82,500	5.09
Estimated 2025		140,000	
2050		190,000	

Source : The Institute of Chartered Accountants of India, New Delhi.

Table 5.4 : Membership of the Institute of Chartered Accountants of India on 1st April 1990

Category of Membership	Fellows	Associates	Total
In Full-time Practice	18,303	17,061	35,364
In Part-time Practice	1,979	6,083	8,062
Not in Practice	1,854	13,718	15,752
Total	22,136	36,862	58,998

Source : The Institute of Chartered Accountants of India, New Delhi.

For promoting international and regional cooperation a number of steps have been taken. The Institute became a founder member of the Confederation of Asian and Pacific Accountants (CAPA) in 1976. In 1977 when the International Federation of Accountants (IFAC) was formed India was elected to the IFAC Council. In 1984 the Institute became the founder member of the South Asian Federation of Accountants (SAFA).

The Institute of Cost & Works Accountants of India

The Institute of Cost & Works Accountants of India (ICWA), a national body of cost accountants in India was set up on 28th May 1959 through an Act of Parliament (Act 23 of 1959). Prior to this a body 'The Indian Institute of Cost & Works Accountants' was set up in 1944 as a limited company under the Companies Act, 1913, which got merged with the Institute when it was set up. The national headquarter of the Institute is at 12, Sudder Street, Calcutta. The Institute has also set up four regional headquarters at Bombay, Delhi, Calcutta and Chennai. Shri R.J. Goel was president, Shri Kunal Banerjee vice president and Shri D. Jagannathan secretary of the Institute for 1999. (SAFA Handbook, 1999 p.24)

The Central Council of the Institute consists of 12 elected members and 4 members are nominated by the Central Government to represent government and academic institutions.

A person of 17 years and above in age and holding bachelor degree from an Indian university or one considered equivalent to it is eligible for registration as a student with the Institute. Persons who have passed senior secondary examination (10+2) have to qualify at the Foundation examination. For new entrants to the profession the Institute conducts Foundation, Intermediate and Final examinations. The students have to undergo mandatory coaching, either postal coaching or oral coaching at a recognized centre. Study material is given to the students opting for correspondence coaching. Though there is no time limit regarding the number of attempts allowed at the examinations but as the registration remains valid for 7 years, if a candidate does not pass the course in 7 years time he has to register again. Examinations of the ICWA foundation, intermediate and final courses are conducted by the Institute twice a year in June and December months. There is no grading system but marks are awarded at the examinations. A student securing 40 per cent or more marks in individual papers and 50 per cent or more marks in the aggregate is declared as pass at the examinations. There is no system of joining training as a student. The position regarding enrolment of students for the ICWA examinations is given in Table 5.5. It may be seen that the enrolment of students for the

ICWA examinations has grown steadily from 7,068 in 1968-69 to 21,065 in 1987-88.

Table 5.5 : Students Enrolled for the ICWA of India Examinations

Year	Number of Students Enrolled	Average Annual Growth Number	%
1968-69	7,068	–	–
1973-74	13,783	+ 1,343	14.3
1978-79	22,278	+ 1,699	10.1
1983-84	37,856	+ 3,116	11.1
1984-85	25,062	-12,794	- 34
1985-86	18,744	- 6,318	- 25
1986-87	18,344	- 400	- 2
1987-88	21,065	+ 2,721	15

Source : Annual Reports of ICWA of India, Calcutta.

The membership of the Institute consists of 'associate' and 'fellow' members. The Institute had over 18,000 associate/ fellow members in 1998, of whom around 2,000 were whole time in practice as cost auditors, management consultants etc. The growth in the membership of the Institute is shown in Table 5.6.

Table 5.6 : Members of the Institute of Cost & Works Accountants of India

Year	Total Members (as on 1st April)	Average Annual Growth Number	%
1944	25	–	–
1960	433	26	20.9
1970	2,272	184	18.4
1980	4,804	253	7.8
1985	6,018	243	4.6
1986	6,405	387	6.4
1987	6,853	448	7.0
1988	7,438	585	8.5

Source : Annual Reports of ICWA of India, Calcutta.

For professional development of the members the Institute conducts seminars, symposia, workshops etc. at different centres on regular basis. It publishes a monthly journal 'The Management Accountant' from Calcutta.

Thus the two bodies of professional accountants organize the education and training for their membership and also regulate the profession. These bodies also undertake for their members continuing education and professional development programmes.

The universities and colleges in India also extend cooperation in organizing oral coaching and conducting the examinations. Some professional development programmes are also organized with the support of educational institutions where the professional accountants as well as the teachers from universities participate.

Nepal

Nepal had no national body of professional accountants for a long time. Persons registered for undertaking audit work of the companies were members of either the Institute of Chartered Accountants of India or the Institute of Chartered Accountants in England. The Institute of Chartered Accountants of India had set up an examination centre at Kathmandu. Some cost accountants, that were members of the Institute of Cost & Works Accountants of India, were also working as professional accountants in Nepal and they had set up a branch of the Institute there. However, now Nepal has a national body of professional accountants in the Institute of Chartered Accountants of Nepal.

Institute of Chartered Accountants of Nepal

The Institute of Chartered Accountants of Nepal was set up in 1998 and is still in early stage of growth. All its existing associate and fellow members are former members of the Institute of Chartered Accountants of India or the Institute of Chartered Accountants of England and Wales. The Institute's headquarter is located at Babar Mahal, POB 5289, Kathmandu, Nepal. Shri Tirth Raj Upadhyay was the president of the Institute with Shri Kaushalendra Kumar Singh as vice president and Shri Purusottam Lal Shrestha as secretary for 1999. (SAFA Handbook, 1999 p.31)

A Memorandum of Understanding was signed between the Institute of Chartered Accountants of India and the Institute of Chartered Accountants of Nepal in 1998, whereby the Institute of Chartered Accountants of Nepal continues to receive full cooperation from the Institute of Chartered Accountants of India in the matters of education, training and examinations. (*Economic Times*)

Pakistan

Soon as Pakistan became independent in 1947 the need for some suitable arrangement for the education, training and examinations for professional accountants and regulation of the profession was realized. Under the Companies Act in force at that time only Registered Accountants were allowed to act as auditors of public companies. A person who satisfied the conditions laid down under the Rules as to both practical training and theoretical knowledge was considered qualified to have his name placed on the register of auditors maintained by the government. These persons were allowed to use the designation 'Registered Accountant'. The period of training for 'article clerks' was 3 to 5 years and those with longer period were known as 'audit clerks'. For testing the knowledge of these persons, two examinations, first examination and second examination, were held. In 1952 the Registered Accountants formed a body named 'Pakistan Institute of Accountants'. In June 1952 the Department of Accounting was set up in the Government of Pakistan with the Controller of Accounts as its head. The Institute of Chartered Accountants of Pakistan was set up on 1st July 1961, with its headquarter in Karachi.

In Pakistan there are three bodies of professional accountants, viz., the Institute of Chartered Accountants of Pakistan, the Institute of Cost & Management Accountants of Pakistan and the Institute of Taxation Management of Pakistan. Each of the above institution has its independent set up for education, training and professional regulation and development of their members. A brief description of the first two is given here.

The Institute of Chartered Accountants of Pakistan

The Institute of Chartered Accountants of Pakistan is the premier body of professional accountants. Its headquarter is situated at

G-31/8, Kehkashan, Clifton, Karachi. Mr. Najam Choudhary, FCA was president, Mr. Mujahid Eshai, FCA and Mr. Pir Mohammed A. Kaliya, FCA were two vice presidents and Mr. A Rashid Chaudhary was secretary of the Institute for 1999. (SAFA Handbook, 1999 p. 15) The affairs of the Institute are managed by the Council which is composed of 16 members, 12 of which are elected and 4 nominated by the Government to represent the Federal Ministries of Finance, Education, Commerce and Industry. Detailed information about the Institute may be obtained from the site www.icap.org.

Apart from regulation of the profession the Institute makes arrangement for the training of new entrants through its members and conducts examinations. The qualification for new entrants up to 30th June 1999 was graduate degree or an equivalent with 18 years or more in age. As per new regulations a person who is HSC/A Level (10+2) can join CA full-time foundation course for 2 years duration after passing pre-entry proficiency test and thereafter passing the foundation course can join as CA student and trainee. The university graduates (10+2+2) of any discipline are allowed to appear at pre-entry proficiency test and on qualifying join as student and trainee. Persons qualifying at foundation examination from the UK are given exemption in some papers. Two examinations, Professional-I and Professional-II are required to be passed during this period. The Institute conducts the examinations twice a year. Grades are awarded at the examinations and for qualifying the candidate should obtain either grade A-Excellent or grade B-Pass.

The period of training earlier was 4 years for commerce graduates and 5 years for non-commerce graduates. Now it is 4 years for all. A trainee has to enter into an agreement with a practicing chartered accountant for training. The duration of industrial training is six months. During this period the trainees are exposed to practical accounting and audit work in industry under the supervision of some chartered accountant in industry. The principal has to give a training report on the completion of training.

For academic instruction the Institute has a system of postal coaching. Oral coaching classes are also organized at selected centres. AT Foulks Lynch and PB Publications provide approved

study material for the courses of the Institute. The principal with whom the student is attached for training has to bear 50 per cent of the cost of this material.

The number of students appearing at the above examinations and qualifying is given in Table 5.7.

Table 5.7 : Candidates Appearing and Qualifying at the Examinations of ICAP

Year	No. of Candidates Appearing		No. of Candidates Qualifying	
	Intermediate	Final	Intermediate	Final
1984	1,455	470	203	50
1985	1,470	614	309	48
1986	1,535	760	227	16
1987	1,582	945	176	17
1988	521	528	52	34

Source : The Institute of Chartered Accountants of Pakistan, Karachi.

The members of the profession are placed in two categories, 'associates' and 'fellows'. A person of 21 years or more in age and qualifying at the CA professional examination on completion of training becomes eligible for the associate membership of the Institute. An associate member of the Institute in practice for 5 years or as associate member for 10 years or more becomes eligible for fellow membership. Members of the Institute of Chartered Accountants of England and Wales, Ireland, Scotland, Australia and Canada are also allowed to apply for the membership of the Institute. The growth in the membership of the Institute is shown in Table 5.8. It may be seen that the Institute had 194 members at the time of its establishment in 1961. As on 1st July 1990 the Institute had 1,416 members, of whom 820 were fellow members and 596 were associate members. The number of members in practice was 268 fellows and 71 associates and 552 fellows and 525 associates were in service.

Table 5.8 : Membership of the Institute of Chartered Accountants of Pakistan

Year	Fellows	Associates	Total
1985	–	–	1,147
1986	–	–	1,203
1987	–	–	1,236
1988	–	–	1,294
1990	820	596	1,416

Source : The Institute of Chartered Accountants of Pakistan, Karachi.

For professional development of members the Institute conducts seminars, symposia and short term courses on subjects of professional interest. The Institute maintains libraries at the headquarter and also at the regional centres for the benefit of members and students. A quarterly journal 'The Pakistan Accountant' and a monthly 'Newsletter' is also published.

The Institute of Cost & Management Accountants of Pakistan

The Institute of Cost & Management Accountants of Pakistan, a body of cost and management accountants in Pakistan was set up in 1951. Later on to give it statutory recognition the Cost & Management Accountants Act was passed in 1966. It was revised in 1990. The headquarter of the Institute is located at ST-18/C, Block-6, Gulshan-e-Iqbal Karachi. Detailed information about the Institute may be obtained from its site www.icmap.com.

A Council as supreme authority runs the affairs of the Institute. The Council comprises of 12 members, 4 being government nominees and 8 elected. It has a president, a vice president, a secretary and a treasurer as office bearers. The Institute has 10 branches located in important towns of the country. Dr. Khawaja Amjad Saeed, FCMA, FCA was president, Mr. Maudood A. Lodhi, FCMA vice president and Mr. M.H. Asif, FCMA secretary of the Institute in 1999.

For new entrants the requirement of educational qualification is bachelor degree (10+2+2) and qualifying at the entry test. Method of academic instructions is both postal coaching and oral coaching. Oral coaching classes are organized at selected centres. The Institute conducts the examinations for ICMA Part I, II, III, IV and V, twice a year with six months gap. The period at each stage of examination is 2 years and if a candidate fails to qualify he has to take admission again and also complete the coaching. Coaching is provided either at accredited coaching centres or through correspondence. Students joining oral coaching are required to attend 75 per cent of the classes. The postal coaching candidates are required to submit 100 per cent assignments.

There is no apprenticeship scheme for the students. Students are expected to work in some commercial/industrial organisation and acquire the necessary experience in the field.

The Institute has two types of membership, associates and fellows. A student qualifying at the ICMAP examination with 3 years practical experience of management accounting becomes eligible for associate membership and an associate member for 5 years who holds a position of chief accountant, chief cost and management accountant or an equivalent post becomes eligible for enrolment for fellow membership. Members of CIMA (the UK) and SMA (Canada) are eligible for the membership of the Institute. The position of the membership of the Institute is given in Table 5.9. It may be seen that the membership of the Institute was 947 in 1991 as against 803 in 1987.

Table 5.9 : Membership of the Institute of Cost & Management Accountants of Pakistan

Year	Number of Members
1987	803
1988	836
1989	869
1990	896
1991	947

Source : The Institute of Cost & Management Accountants of Pakistan, Karachi.

Sri Lanka

In Sri Lanka there is only one national body of professional accountants, the Institute of Chartered Accountants of Sri Lanka. The Institute is member of the South Asian Federation of Accountants.

The Institute of Chartered Accountants of Sri Lanka

The Institute of Chartered Accountants of Sri Lanka is the premier body of professional accountants in Sri Lanka. The headquarter of the Institute is located at 30A, Malalasekera Mawatha, Colombo. Mr. Nanayakkara, FCA, BA was president, Mr. Ranel T. Wijesinha, FCA, MBA vice president and Mr. Lakshman Perera Secretary of the Institute in 1999. (SAFA

Handbook, 1999 p.50) Detailed information about the Institute may be obtained from the site www.lanka.net/ica.

A graduate (10+2+2) from any university in Sri Lanka or any other university recognised as equivalent and approved by the Council can join as registered student. Candidates qualifying at the foundation examination of the CIMA (the UK), ACCA (the UK), ICSA (the UK) and AIA (the UK) are also eligible for enrolment. The Institute holds oral coaching through lecture method for its students. Alternatively a student can join the correspondence course. For its foundation, intermediate and final students the Institute holds examinations twice a year. Maximum 5 attempts are allowed for foundation and 8 attempts for the intermediate examination. There is no restriction of attempts for the final examination. There is no grading system but marks are awarded at the examinations.

For the training of new entrants the Institute has made arrangement with its members. A student has to enter into an agreement with a practicing chartered accountant for this purpose. The period of training is 4 years, 2 years leading to intermediate level and 2 years leading to final level.

The Institute has two types of members, associate members and fellow members. A person on qualifying at the final examination and completing the training becomes eligible for associate membership of the Institute. An associate member acquiring the required CPE credits becomes eligible for fellow membership of the Institute. An associate or a fellow member having practical training for 2 years or more with some practicing chartered accountant may apply for certificate of practice.

Thus five countries out of seven member countries of SAARC, viz., India, Pakistan, Bangladesh, Nepal and Sri Lanka have set up national bodies of professional accountants, which conduct examinations for membership and regulate the profession. The bodies of professional accountants also organize continuing education and professional development programmes for their members.

The universities and colleges also extend cooperation in organizing oral coaching and in conducting the examinations. Some professional development programmes are also organized with the support of educational institutions where the professional accountants as well as the teachers from universities participate.

There are certain differences in respect of arrangement for enrolment, qualification for new entrants, system of coaching, courses of study, examinations, training etc. from one country to another. But gradually there is an effort to learn from each other's experience and improve. The existing arrangement worked satisfactorily to an extent in the past. However, with the winds of globalization blowing all over the world their systems are under strain and need revamping.

Education of Government Accountants

A system through which the planning, control and accountability functions of the government are carried out is known as government accounting. Government accounting being an adjunct of public administration is inspired by political philosophy of the state. In Asian countries the system has a strong philosophical basis.

Though the basic principles are the same the government accounting is different from commercial accounting in practice in several ways. Greater emphasis is placed upon compliance with rules and regulations, propriety and public interest in it. (Sharma, IJA June, 1997) Government accounting is done under the supervision and control of government authorities at different levels, within the overall legislative and statutory control.

The education and training of government accountants is responsibility of the governments. Accordingly arrangement is made at different levels and in different departments. Generally specialized training centres are set up for this purpose. Similar training centres are set for the accountants in public sector, such as insurance and banking sector companies. Practical training is given while working on the job. Certain examinations are also organized for promotion from lower cadres to higher cadres.

The Constitution of India has installed the Comptroller and Auditor General of India (CAG) as a high, independent statutory authority. It is the constitutional duty of the CAG to ensure that the expenses voted by the Parliament/Legislature are not exceeded or varied, the funds available are used properly and proper accounts are maintained in respect of revenue and expenditure. Apart from his other functions the CAG supervises the training arrangement for the government accountants. A similar arrangement exists in other SAARC member countries also.

The accounts of the Royal Government of Bhutan are maintained by different government departments as per the provisions of the Financial Manual issued by the Ministry of Finance on the recommendation of the Royal Audit Authority, Thimpu. The Revenue and Customs Divisions under the Ministry of Finance deal with the matters regarding taxation as per the rules made in this respect. The Companies Act of 1985 has provisions regarding maintenance of books of accounts and audit. These are applicable to companies in public sector as well as in private sector.

Accounting and accountability have been essential features of Nepalese culture and social life. With a view to satisfying high expectations an institution with high religious and moral authority, known as Kumari Chowk was established in 1771. All public accounts were submitted to Kumari Chowk for audit. This arrangement continued up to 1959, when the office of Auditor General of Nepal came into existence. The Auditor General of Nepal is a constitutional authority appointed by His Majesty the King of Nepal for a period of six years. Accounting and audit functions have been separated and now while the government accounts are maintained by the Department of the Accountant General of Nepal, audit is done by the Department of Auditor General of Nepal. This audit is comprehensive and due consideration is given to regulatory, austerity, efficiency, effectiveness as well as propriety aspects. The Auditor General submits a report on work done to His Majesty the King of Nepal every year, which is then placed before the Rastriya Panchayat. (Sharma, 1987) The education of senior officers of the state in accounts cadre is done at the Institute of Public Administration at Kathmandu.

Similar arrangement for the training of the government accountants exists in other member countries of SAARC. Over the years in tune with the changing requirement of financial control, audit control and legislative control the system of government accounting is also being modified. In most of these countries the officers are selected through open competition and trained. There exists separate cadre of officers and other personnel of account service.

Education and Training of Global Accountant

If the eighties were the age of computers, nineties the age of information technology, the first decade of the next millennium would be the age of knowledge. The intellectual capital shall drive the organizations. The quality and success of the organization shall be determined by the quality of human resources or the intellectual capital.

In the highly surcharged and competitive environment the quality will hold the key to an individual's future. The accounting education programmes should, therefore, be fine-tuned to prepare the students of accounting to become professionals in the true sense. To attain and maintain the status of a professional accountant life long learning shall be required. The base on which life long learning can be built should have three components: skills, knowledge and professional orientation. (AECC, S-1, 1990 pp.1-3)

It may be pertinent here to quote from the statements of the Accounting Education Change Commission to put the position in clearer perspective. It has been mentioned in the Statement 1 that to become a successful professional accountant one must possess communication skills, intellectual skills, and interpersonal skills. Accounting graduates should have general knowledge, organizational and business knowledge, and accounting knowledge. Accounting graduates should identify with the profession and be concerned with developing the knowledge, skills and values of its members. They should know and understand the ethics of the profession and be able to make value based judgements. (AECC, S-1 1990 pp.1-3)

Reports of the Review Committees for Accounting Education

For reviewing the system of education and training in the context of changing social and economic scenario the Institute of

Chartered Accountants of India have set up review committees from time to time, in 1959, 1963, 1970, 1972 and in 1975. An inquiry was also conducted in this respect in 1966-68. It may be pertinent to give a brief description of the report of the Review Committee set up in September 1975. The Committee worked over four years (1975-76, 1976-77, 1977-78 and 1978-79), elicited opinions and suggestions from a large group of persons and submitted a detailed report, which was published in 1979. Spread over nine chapters the report covered all important matters affecting the accounting profession in India, which included entry requirement, practical experience, theoretical instructions, examinations, syllabus, continuing education and post-graduate courses.

The report of the Committee formed the basis of the changes made by the ICAI in the whole set up of education and training in 1980s and in 1990s.

Report of Special Committee on Education of Chartered Accountants in Pakistan

Recognizing the need for an in-depth study and review of the current educational system and practical training scheme for the aspiring chartered accountants, the Council of the Institute of Chartered Accountants of Pakistan (ICAP), had in December 1985 constituted a special committee to assess and report "whether the syllabi ensures an appropriate degree of knowledge and expertise expected of a chartered accountant; whether the mode of training effectively caters to the acquisition of required knowledge and skills; what should be the number and interval of examinations to test the knowledge and expertise; whether there should be a maximum number of attempts within which such examinations should be cleared; and whether it is advisable to have different modes of practical training for students opting for industry and those opting for profession or in any other manner with emphasis on specific fields of specialization like Taxation, Cost Accounting, Management Accounting etc." (SCETCA, 1988 p.3)

After extensive studies the Committee submitted the report, which was published in August 1988. Specific recommendations of the Committee in brief were as follows:

(1) There shall be an increasing need of accountants to cater to the expanding economy of the country.
(2) With the changing complexion of business establishments due to the demands of computer age and information explosion, comprehensive training programmes shall be needed to equip the modern accountants.
(3) While the syllabi prescribed seem comprehensive the education and training mechanism of the Institute was inadequate due to poor base of university education, absence of pragmatic policy and non-availability of relevant literature, insufficient time for training, non-serious attitude of examinees and limitless number of attempts allowed to clear the examinations.

The Committee, therefore, recommended that:

(1) Apart from the basic qualifications for entry there should be an aptitude test. For this revival of entrance examinations should be considered.
(2) Comprehensive training should be provided on whole time basis over a period of four years to new entrants.
(3) Considering the desirability of producing accounting technicians the Committee recommended that either this should be left to subsidiary associations under the patronage of the Institute as in England and Sri Lanka or it may be taken up either by the Institute or a body recognized by it.

Arrangement in Developed Countries

It may be pertinent to mention here that the SAARC countries can learn a lot regarding accounting education from the developed countries, particularly from the UK and the USA.

In the UK there are four bodies of professional accountants, viz., the Association of Book Keepers, the Association of Chartered Certified Accountants (ACCA), the Association of Chartered Accountants (ACA) and the Association of Cost and Management Accountants (ACMA), each with a specific role. The Association of book keepers prepares accounting personnel for jobs at lower level, while the Association of Chartered

Certified Accountants prepares accounting personnel for middle level. Members of the Association of Chartered Accountants work as auditors and the members of the Association of Cost and Management Accountants work as cost accountants.

The Association of bookkeepers and the Association of Chartered Certified Accountants have liaison with polytechnics and many private educational institutions by giving them accreditation for preparing the students for their examinations.

In the USA there is no national accountancy law. There are 52 states and within each state's jurisdiction the state laws establish the right to practice as a professional accountant through a licensing procedure. In some cases by law, whereas in other cases this requirement is established by a rule making body, usually a state board of accountancy, has laid down specific qualifications. Most professional accountants are members of a state society a body of accountants, which sets membership requirements, and the rules of conduct that govern the actions of professional accountants.

To address the multiple jurisdiction problem in 1990 a special American Institute of Certified Public Accountants (AICPA) Committee on Governance and Structure had recommended a national qualification service to establish and administer qualifications for individuals for licensing. (Needles, 1999 p.3)

The American Institute of Certified Public Accountants exercises indirect regulatory influence over the qualifications of the accountants through its membership requirement, the uniform CPA examination, and a national test conducted and graded by it.

Accountancy education is subjected to national regulation through the accreditation standards imposed by the American Assembly of Collegiate Schools of Business in the United States.

Suggestions for Upgrading the System of Education and Training

In the background of the reports of two Committees and the framework in some other countries given above some suggestions are given here for upgrading the system of education and training of professional accountants in the SAARC countries.

1. Curriculum Development

Dramatic changes are being experienced in the field of accounting due to rapid pace of technological changes. The ability to retain the competitive advantage by a society depends upon its ability to educate. The existing syllabus of the CA and CWA/CMA examinations are basically tuned to meet the requirement of traditional functions of accountants such as corporate accounting, corporate audit and taxation in case of CAs and cost accounting, cost control and cost audit in case of CWAs/CMAs, whereas the world of accounting and finance is changing very fast. A variety of new areas have emerged and are expected to emerge, which shall require the expertise of professional accountants such as E-commerce, E-banking, E-stock market trading, forex transactions, portfolio management, project consultancy, financial services, multinational accounting, international financial management, innovative financial instruments etc.

Under the circumstances for effective teaching innovative curriculum and course development need great emphasis. An increased emphasis on teaching and curriculum and course development is vital to the future of professional accounting education. (AECC S-1, Aug. 1990, pp.1-2)

Like universities the bodies of professional accountants enjoy freedom to formulate curriculum for their examinations. However, this should be done after in-depth research and wider consultations. Greater depth and also breadth to cover a variety of specializations should be provided. Flexibility should also be provided in the syllabus to take care of the fast changing scenario, so that modifications may be done without procedural hassles. The expertise available with the universities should be utilised for this purpose.

2. Arrangement for Teaching

The existing arrangement made by the bodies of professional accountants in different countries for education of the students enrolled is based on distance learning or postal coaching mode and limited oral coaching is conducted. It is already under strain due to expanding numbers. It is not the best arrangement for professional education. For Accounting subjects, where personal interaction with the faculty and laboratory work are involved it is not be possible to arrange for the teaching of these subjects through postal coaching. It may, therefore, be suggested that specialized schools of accounting should be established on the pattern of the management schools. (Sharma, 1997 p.4) Such an arrangement already exists in the USA and the results have been satisfactory.

In this process to begin with some university departments/private institutions in metropolitan towns and large cities may be accredited for teaching the courses. At the same time some specialized institutes for accountants should be set up on the pattern of the IIMs and IITs in India. High quality academics and professionals should be invited to serve as faculty on full-time basis at these institutions. They may be offered salary package comparable with what consulting assignments offer. They should further be offered flexible time schedule for teaching, research and consultancy for greater commitment. These centres may serve as Centres of Excellence. At a later stage more such centres may be established, as per local conditions and on demand, on the same pattern.

3. Examination System

The institutes of professional accountants in the SAARC countries generally conduct bi-annual examinations. It is a massive exercise, since a large number of students appear at the examinations. However, the success rate at these examinations is low. As a result at each level the students make repeated attempts to qualify at the examinations. Apart from causing avoidable agony to young minds, it creates pressure on the examination infrastructure due to larger numbers. It is a wasteful activity in case of those who have to finally leave. It is also observed that sometimes even some weak students also are able to qualify through coaching and repeated attempts. It should be prevented and the maximum number of attempts allowed at each stage should be fixed.

Foundation examinations are organised by some institutes for new entrants from school system. This was also expected to be a filtering screen so that the students who may not be expected to do well later may be weeded out at the first point. However, it is observed that at this stage also some students try to qualify through private tuition and repeated attempts. Allowing repeated attempts at foundation examination defeats the very purpose for which they were provided. The number of attempts allowed in case of foundation examinations should not exceed two.

4. Professional Development

It is an important duty of the body of professional accountants to make arrangement for the training and professional development of the members on continuing basis. This is necessary to remain contemporary in every respect so far as the professional knowledge is concerned. In the past, since the pace of change was slow, it was not given higher priority. But with rapid changes in the organizations, their working styles, technology etc. this should receive very high priority. Such an arrangement for professional accountants should include upgrading the skills required for interfacing the clients, with firms, with government authorities and regulatory bodies, remaining updated with the global practices, use of information technology etc. For this the bodies of professional accountants should lay greater emphasis upon and provide more time and resources for the organisation of seminars and workshops. Credits should be given for attending these programmes. Minimum requirement should be specified and made mandatory for all members.

5. Professional Ethics and Code of Conduct

Professional ethics and code of conduct are mechanism for disciplining professional persons. Ethics is the study of human behaviour based on philosophical speculation, whereas the code of conduct is a set of rules governing the conduct of a group of persons. Compliance with ethics is based on morality, whereas the code of conduct is a professional requirement enforced through rules. However, the idea behind both is the same, to maintain the sanctity of the profession and inspire confidence in public so far as the members of a profession are concerned. In case of growth of a profession ethics is the first casualty. With increasing numbers there may be increasing difficulties in maintaining ethical values and enforcing the code of conduct.

As young minds crave for knowledge and make sincere efforts for the advancement of learning and strive for excellence it is the duty of educators and seniors to help them to cultivate and develop technical skills required for excelling and at the same time to teach and enforce ethical values, for the very existence of the profession depends upon ethical behaviour.

It is a happy feature that the bodies of professional accountants in all the SAARC countries subscribe to a code of conduct. This is used for disciplining the members of the profession. There have been a number of cases in India where the ICAI had taken action against the members for the violation of the code of conduct.

However, the crux of the problem is enforcement. It should be the duty of every member of the profession to guard the honour of the profession fiercely. All violations of the code of conduct should be brought to the knowledge of the Institute and appropriate action should be taken in each case.

Conclusions

In conclusion it may be stated that the existing arrangement for education and training of professional accountants in the SAARC countries is to an extent going well. The national bodies of professional accountants have established a useful framework and network within the country and also at regional and international level. However, with globalisation the nature and extent of challenge faced by a professional accountant is also expected to grow. It would, therefore, be necessary to make changes in the framework from time to time so that it may deal effectively with the changing requirements of the profession.

Every country has its unique environment and problems, and all the countries of the world can adopt a single model howsoever good it may be. However, some of the features, which may be considered suitable, may certainly be adopted. In this respect the features like arrangement for education of new entrants with the association of universities, professional development of the members through joint seminars, effective monitoring of the activities of the members of the profession, effective enforcement of code of conduct etc. should certainly be emphasized upon.

The bodies of professional accountants in the SAARC countries should establish a strong liaison with the universities, colleges and other educational institutions in their countries on long term basis. They should seek their cooperation in developing curriculum, organising education of young entrants, conduct of examinations, organising joint seminars and continuing education programmes for the members. This should be based on mutuality of interest.

6

SUMMARY, CONCLUSIONS AND GUIDELINES FOR ACTION

Summary

Education plays a vital role in the process of development and also in improvement of quality of life for individuals as well as the society as a whole. Recognizing this governments in all the countries strive to raise the quality and the level of education.

Flow of funds from international financial institutions, inter-country economic assistance and investment by private sector are essential for economic development, apart from the basic effort from the government. In the process of development, accounting education provides the foundation for the regulatory mechanism/control systems and practices, which may ensure economic fairness and efficiency on the one hand and fulfil the requirement of accountability on the other.

Seven countries of South Asia have formed an association for regional cooperation known as South Asian Association for Regional Cooperation (SAARC), to involve cooperation in solving the problems specific to the region, strengthen collective self-reliance and accelerate economic, social and cultural development. All these countries are close neighbours and have a long history, a common cultural heritage and strong religious and cultural affinity.

The research project 'Accounting Education in the Countries of South Asian Region' has been an exploration of the distinctive features, the social systems, the economies, the education systems and the arrangement for accounting education under the university system and also by the bodies of professional accountants.

Important findings of the research have been as under :

1. In spite of adverse political relations, poor infrastructure base, and low level of literacy and income, the SAARC countries are in transition, shifting their focus from agriculture to industry and services. This created good scope for economic cooperation.
2. These countries share a common history and geography. Their economies have great potential to benefit from mutual cooperation. However, inter-country trade and commerce have not developed to satisfactory level. Trade barriers persist. The efforts made towards establishing the South Asian Free Trade Area and other forums for economic cooperation have not made much progress.
3. All these countries are, however, experiencing flow of 'foreign investment' and their economies are slowly moving towards economic integration with the rest of the world.
4. There has been significant growth in education including higher education in the SAARC countries during the last fifty years, though the state of literacy still remains very low. These countries have not been able to make significant achievement in terms of human development. Most of these countries are placed at the lowest level, as compared to other countries in the ranking.
5. Under the influence of socialistic ideals a major share of the expenditure on education at all stages has been borne by the governments and the fees charged from the beneficiaries have been kept low. However, the governments are gradually withdrawing funding support to higher education. It is suggested that the users and the beneficiaries should share the cost of higher education. This shall require a radical change in the concept as well as the strategy of higher education including business education.
6. Though over the years much improvement has come there is a wider criticism of university commerce education in general including accounting education. It is often men-

tioned that it does not adequately equip the students with required technical and specialized skills.

7. While the role of accounting is well recognized and the work of professional accountants has been given a legal status in most of the countries, accounting has not been recognized as a separate discipline under the university system in the region.
8. With the changing complexion of business, expanding international trade there has been increasing scope for professional accountants. However, the system of education and training has not measured up to the expectation due to poor base, lack of quality education, absence of pragmatic policy, insufficient exposure of the new entrants to real life situations.

Modern accounting systems had their origin and growth under the aegis of the mercantile school of economics, which stood for capitalist economy, unrestricted private gain and non-participation and non-interference by the state in business. At a later stage under the influence of welfare school and socialist ideology the emphasis shifted to public sector enterprises with huge investment in basic and heavy industries with social objectives. Accounting systems had to change to protect public interest. Now once again the emerging concept of globalized economy has brought about a shift in emphasis upon efficiency and quality of product and service. This has necessitated economic reforms, fiscal policy changes, financial sector reforms, trade liberalization and a variety of other initiatives by governments, financial institutions and business. This would require establishment of efficient accounting information system for internal and external reporting and control, greater accountability, rigorous system of audit and disclosure norms.

With the growth of international trade and commerce the transactions involving foreign exchange are expected to increase in numbers as well as complexity. This would require dynamic accounting professionals who may effectively deal with such complex matters. With expanding international economic and financial contacts the coverage of the international aspects of accounting, such as international accounting standards, harmonization of international accounting practices, international audit guidelines etc. shall require increased attention.

The accounting education and the profession have to grow in conformity with the present day economic and social needs. It is equally important to bear in mind that the improvement in the technical competence of the practitioners have enabled them to bear heavier responsibilities of dealing with business problems in an overall context, with integrity, independence, transparency and accountability.

Problems and Challenges

To equip the future accountants to face these challenges there is a need for strengthening the training and education of accounting with greater emphasis on research and development.

A new millennium is approaching. This is a very important time in the history of modern civilization. This event means a number of things, which may affect all of us in different ways. While the accountants shall have an important role even in the next century the profile of the work done by them and the way they carry it out is expected to change. For instance, the corporate audit shall become highly complex. The auditor may be called upon to track high tech frauds, miss-appropriations and financial scandals requiring newer strategies for tackling these white-collar crimes. Likewise in taxation instead of routine filling of returns and payment of tax, advance tax projections, tax planning and tax management may become more important. These shall require high quality knowledge and proficiency.

Some of the trends clearly visible on the horizon are :

Social Changes – Growing Middle Class and Entry of Women

The middle class, who form the backbone of the society, is growing in all the countries of the world, including in South Asia, in numbers as well as in economic strength. A large number of students entering higher education including business education come from this class. The career ambition of this class of students is high and they join education programmes that are expected to offer higher salary package and better social status.

With the change in social structure it is also observed that an increasingly larger number of women are joining higher education including professional education. They have proved themselves good learners and competent professional persons. They compete with men for higher level jobs on merit. Accounting skills are sex neutral and provide a good career for women. In the long run this may change the profile of the profession and maybe some of the problems the profession is facing shall be automatically solved. At the same time the education and training arrangement must also be equipped considering this aspect.

Expansion of Work and New Job Opportunities

The scope of accounting has expanded a great deal over the last 50 years. It is expected to grow and expand further with liberalization and globalization of the economies, emergence of the WTO, growth of multinational companies, interdependence of economies etc. In the wake of market economy a variety of expertise shall be required. For instance, professional expertise shall be required for project formulation and implementation, designing financial structure and raising funds from market for companies, designing and implementing schemes of mergers and takeovers, capital market operations, foreign exchange transactions etc. This would mean more opportunities and more work for professional accountants. However, this is expected to put pressure on the existing infrastructure, unless urgent attention is given to this problem.

Speculation and insider trading have been the bane of stock markets in the past. With electronic trading it has been possible to exercise effective control over the functioning of these markets. However, at the same time the stock market operations have become highly complex and risky. It may be difficult for individual investors to operate in stock market in future without the support of research, investment advisers, consultant's etc. This throws open a new field of activity for accounting professionals.

Changes in Job Requirements

The preference of young persons for jobs generally changes like the change in fashion. For instance in fifties and sixties there was a marked preference for civil services and public sector. In the eighties it changed to accounting, business management, engineering and medicine, and in the nineties to finance, electronics, information technology, media and computers.

In the next millennium the focus seem to be shifting towards service sector, information technology, entertainment, hospitality, consultancy, insurance, banking, international trade, foreign exchange markets etc. The best of talent are expected to be attracted to jobs in these areas, and these areas are expected to be highly challenging as well as rewarding.

It may mean that accounting profession, which has been an area of choice for young persons, may not be able to attract the best talent and to that extent the growth of the profession may suffer unless the professionals equip themselves for new specialisations.

Inter-Disciplinary Education

In the past corporate accounting and corporate audit were the areas of core competence of the professional accountants. Professional accountants were preferred for the positions of Comptrollers, Treasurers, Internal Auditors, though the majority among them established their own professional firms and took up statutory audit of accounts of companies and firms. They maintained a distinct identity and class character. At a later stage taxation became an important area, where they excelled as tax planners and tax practitioners. Some years back the area of management services attracted them, where their knowledge of accounting and finance was considered useful for making organizations more effective in their operations.

Though each person selects a particular area for himself out of the alternatives, yet the professional accountants have to deal with a number of different activities and are expected to be multi-skilled professionals. Thus while accounting audit and taxation have remained the main areas of specialization for the accountants the way they have carried it out have changed over the years. It may further change in the wake of globalization. For instance the auditors are already using modern technology in audit work. So is the case with accounting, tax planning, tax consultancy, investment planning and portfolio management etc. Gradually the information technology is getting integrated with the hardcore accounting work.

Invasion of Technology

Over the last two decades tremendous developments have taken place in technology, which has come to constitute an important and inevitable component of higher education in many developed countries. (Shah, 1986 p.3) With computers and other electronic aids replacing the age-old systems of maintaining files, books of accounts, memorizing sums etc., the entire accounting environment is expected to change. Invisible accounting is replacing the visible accounting. The capability, the speed and the efficiency in information processing, analysis, retrieval and presentation has gone up considerably. Security of accounting information has also become a significant factor.

The technological changes will create their own problems and shall require new types of skills and technical competence to meet effectively the challenge. To successfully face the unfolding scenario and harness technology, the education and training of the modern accountant must be considerably upgraded. In this respect it may be suggested that use of computers in day to day operations must increase. Computer should form an essential tool in the kit of a modern accountant. Special training programmes should be designed for the professional accountants whether in service or in practice both. The requirement and the guidance in respect of audit evidence, vouchers, test checking etc., should be redesigned in the light of the requirement of this new technology.

Multinational Accounting

The market forces are expected to impact the accounting profession in a big way. Changes in business organisations such as restructuring organizations, mergers and acquisitions etc. are expected to pose certain problems. Globalization has already prompted big accounting firms/foreign entities with strong brand image and logo to extend their reach all over the globe for rendering their services. The SAARC countries are no exception. However, in the long run the situation is expected to favour smaller firms rather than larger firms, provided they keep pace with the changes taking place and mature into competent firms and ensure quality service with personal touch to their clients. This could be possible only if they adopt the internationally acceptable practices, norms and standards.

Accounting education is subject to little regulation at international level. However, gradually the regional bodies like Federation of European Accountants (FEA), Confederation of Asian and Pacific Accountants (CAPA) etc. are becoming stronger. The United Nations exerted its influence especially through the International Working Group of Experts on International Standards of Accounting and Reporting (ISAR). The WTO Working Group on Professional services has brought out a draft paper on "Guidelines for Mutual Recognition Agreements or Arrangements in the Accounting Sector." Following these developments UNTAD is developing an international benchmark for assessing national accounting credentials to determine whether they meet world standards or not. (Needles, 1999 p.5)

The Education Committee of the International Federation of Accountants (IFAC) have issued International Education Guidelines (IEGs) laying down essential requirements for accounting education, which have the potential for international recognition, acceptance and application. (Needles, 1999 p.7) All these actions are expected to change the flavour of accounting education.

WTO Norms for Trade in Accounting Services

Mutual recognition of registration and qualification of the professionals is done by competent bodies in different countries to enable these professionals to work in their country. Bilateral agreements have to be made for this purpose. However, the differences in education and examination standards, experience requirement, regulatory influence etc. have made recognition on multinational basis extremely difficult. To make it easier for the governments to negotiate agreements on mutual recognition of professional qualifications, the World Trade Organisation's (WTO) Council for Trade in Services has adopted guidelines for mutual recognition agreements (MRAs). These guidelines are non binding. It has been provided under the guidelines that the agreements should specify the mechanism by which the eligibility for such recognition may be established. If the MRA is based on qualifications it should state the minimum level of education required, the minimum level of experience required, examinations to be passed, the qualifications to be recognized, the rules and procedure to be used to monitor and enforce the provisions of the agreements, the mechanism for dialogue and administrative cooperation between the parties and means of arbitration in case of dispute etc. and relevant laws and regulations to be applied, disciplinary jurisdiction, criteria and procedure for revocation of recognition etc. (E.T. May 31, 1997)

In spite of a variety of limitations it is a matter of satisfaction that the SAARC countries have a large number of competent professional accountants. The quality of work done by them has met the tests of national as well as international standards. These countries should, therefore, enter into MRAs to enable the professional accountants of their countries to work in other countries also.

Guidelines for Action

It has been observed that the efforts directed at revamping the accounting education have proceeded so far either on individual university/department basis or on state basis, with limited interaction with other universities and the bodies of professional accountants. Similarly the bodies of professional accountants have limited interaction with the universities in the matter of curriculum development and professional training. They involve university faculty only in areas where they need manpower support, such as for organizing oral coaching classes or conducting examinations, or for the evaluation of answer papers etc.

There is thus a need for formulating an over all policy for accounting education, pooling resources and working for common objectives, rather than individual objectives. Thus all stakeholders, the executive of the Indian Accounting Association, the Commerce Panel of the University Grants Commission, the Councils of the Institutes of Professional Accountants and the bodies of employers and entrepreneurs, such as the FICCI, the IMA, the CCI etc. should sit together, discuss and evolve an over all policy and a plan of action and work for the common objectives. Some of the issues and problems, which must receive attention of these bodies, are discussed here.

Institute University Coordination

It is a unique feature of accounting education that the students qualifying at the final examination of the Institutes of professional accountants are allowed to be registered as members and are designated as professional accountants, while those qualifying at the masters degree examinations in accounting of the universities are not allowed to be so registered. This position prevails in all the SAARC countries.

It is sometimes suggested that accounting education should be completely shifted to the universities leaving the professional institutes to play the role of a coordinating agency. (Grower, 1998 p.69) Historically academy has made a significant contribution to accounting education including the development of the profession. In the SAARC countries also this has been so. However, with the establishment of the national bodies of professional accountants dichotomy has developed, which has no rationale. A comparison of curriculums of university Commerce courses, such as B.Com., M.Com. etc. and the courses of the professional examinations, such as CA, CWA/CMA etc., reveals that the two are broadly similar in nomenclature of the subjects, content, study material etc. Major difference lies in practical training and legal recognition. (Khandelwal, 1992 p.56)

Accounting educators can learn something from the experience of other countries, particularly the developed countries. For instance in the UK, apart from the conventional Bachelor of Commerce (B.Com.) and Master of Commerce (M.Com.) degrees the universities provide specialized degree in accounting at undergraduate and post-graduate level. The Association of Chartered Accountants and the Association of Cost & Management Accountants recognize these university degrees and exemption is given to the students in some of the papers at the examinations of the Associations.

In this direction it may be suggested that the universities and institutes should support each other and a truly integrated system of education should be developed, the universities and the institutes should jointly design the curriculum, teaching should be done with a professional approach, with required emphasis on theory as well as practice, the university faculty doing teaching and the members of the professional bodies and their clients in business providing training to these students. Such a long term understanding and coordination will go a long way in shaping the new entrants to the profession on sound basis.

A similar arrangement should be worked out between the Institutes of Management (IIMs) on the one hand and the university departments and schools of management on the other. Both should work in close harmony for the development of curriculum, teaching material including cases and sharing the experiences and the education technology.

Arrangement for Quality Assurance

A disturbing feature observed in commerce education including accounting education that has developed in the recent past in certain degree and diploma courses with similar nomenclature and curriculum claiming to be job oriented and professional courses. These are run by university departments, colleges, private institutions, both recognized and non-recognized, institutes of professional accountants, institutes of management etc. Diploma in Foreign Trade, Diploma in Management, Diploma in Corporate Accounting, Diploma in Management Accounting, Diploma in Taxation and Tax Planning are some such examples. A student in such a situation finds it very difficult to decide which one among these is useful and which is not.

In a market oriented economy this cannot be ruled out altogether, and ultimately all these programmes have to prove their utility in the market. However, to put an end to the above avoidable human problem this created some arrangement for national level merit rating and certification should be evolved, which may serve as quality assurance mechanism. The Indian Accounting Association, which has an abiding interest and a unique position as the premier body of academics in accounting, may start such a service.

Inter-Institution Cooperation

The Institute of Chartered Accountants of India have mooted the concept of lateral entry among the professions. It is suggested that the accounting professionals belonging to the Indian Audit and Accounts Service could be offered a CA qualification on qualifying at the examinations of the Institute without going through the process of articleship. Further that they could be allowed exemption at examination in papers, which they have already qualified at the time of qualifying for service. A similar arrangement is suggested in case of the members belonging to different institutes such as ICWA, company secretary etc. (E.T. June 26, 1997) It is a welcome development and should be pursued to its logical conclusions in areas of mutual recognition.

With the growth of trade, commerce and industry professionals with a variety of skills are needed. This created scope for more jobs in these areas. Some of these jobs require multi-disciplinary coordination and involvement. For instance, an auditor working with a specialist technocrat can undertake 'energy audit' or 'environmental audit'. Lateral entry of professionals is expected to solve such problems. For developing multi-skilled professionals such lateral entry can be very useful and should be encouraged.

There has been a demand from some bodies of professional persons for the recognition of their examinations as equivalent to university degrees. For instance the Institute of Chartered

Accountants of India has moved to various universities for recognition of their final examination and membership as equivalent to master degree in Commerce, Accounting and Management, and for considering their members qualified for selection as lecturers in the universities and colleges and also permitting them registration for Ph.D. degree. Some of the universities in India have already accorded recognition to their professional qualifications, ACA and FCA for registration for Ph.D. degree. The All India Institute of Technical Education has recognized the professional qualifications, CA and ICWA for teaching certain management courses. However, in these cases no reciprocity is involved. Without reciprocity and mutual recognition any such arrangement is not expected to last for a long time.

There is already a demand from the members of faculty in the universities and colleges to permit them to enroll as professional accountants, subject to their qualifying at the final examination, granting exemption from articleship. Though the institutes have brushed aside this demand on one argument or the other, but since they have been demanding equivalence with the university degrees and the same has been already given by some of the universities, the demand for according equivalence to university degrees, subject to certain reasonable conditions appears justified.

Inter-Country Cooperation

There are differences in accounting education systems of different countries due to cultural, social and economic differences. There are also inter-institution differences, even within a country. For instance each country has its own system of education and training for accounting personnel. There are differences in respect of minimum qualification for entry and eligibility for examinations, training arrangement, courses of study and examinations. To an extent these differences are inevitable. Yet measures should be undertaken to identify these differences and minimize them to the extent possible. At the same time mutual understanding and respect for the accounting education systems of other countries is essential for inter-country cooperation and for learning from each other's experience.

There is a great scope for inter-country cooperation in accounting education among the SAARC countries. India among these countries has over the last 50 years developed a certain expertise in the field, which could be utilized for mutual benefit.

The Memorandum of Understanding signed in Kathmandu by the President of the Institute of Chartered Accountants of India Mr. Rahul Roy and the President of the Institute of Chartered Accountants of Nepal, Mr. Kamal Chitrakar, whereby the ICAI will help the ICAN to set up its administrative, educational, developmental, technical and regulatory mechanism is an example of such a potential. The ICAI has also been requested by several policy-making bodies in Nepal to assist them in establishing the necessary systems, through the ICA of Nepal.

The ICAI has also initiated a dialogue with the ICA of Bangladesh to assist them in developing and conducting the continuing education programmes for their members. Similar efforts are also going on with Sri Lanka. (E.T. June 26, 1998) It is a welcome development and shall go a long way in developing understanding and bridges between these countries. This is an important objective of SAARC and also a real need of the time. This objective should be pursued with full vigour by the institutes of professional accountants.

APPENDICES

APPENDIX 1.A

ACCOUNTING EDUCATION IN THE COUNTRIES OF SOUTH ASIAN REGION

Questionnaire for Universities

(Faculty of Commerce/Faculty of Management/
Department of Accountancy)

1. Name and complete address of the University:

____

____

____

2. Name and Complete Address of Faculty of Commerce/Faculty of Management/Department of Accounting:

____

____

____

3. Name, Qualifications and Complete Address of Dean/Chairman Faculty

____

____

4. Year of Establishment of Faculty

____

5. Name and Complete Address of Head, Department of Commerce/Accounting/Management

____

____

6. Year of Establishment of Department __________

7. Faculty : Positions, Essential Qualification and Number of Posts.

Position	Essential Qualification	Number of Posts in Faculty of Commerce	Number of Posts in Faculty of Management
a. Professor	______	______	______
b. Assoc. Prof./ Reader	______	______	______
c. Asst. Prof./ Lecturer	______	______	______

Note : Please attach a list of Faculty Members.

8. Academic Institutions with the University:

	Graduate Degree	Post-graduate Degree	Certificate/ Diploma
a. Total Number of Constituent/ Affiliated Colleges	______	______	______
b. Total Number of Institutions/ Colleges Teaching Accounting Courses	______	______	______
c. Total Number of Faculty Members in (a) and (b) above (a)	______	______	______
(b)	______	______	______

9. Number of Scholars on the Rolls of the Faculty (Yearwise)

Course	1951	1961	1971	1981	1991	1995
a. B.Com./BBA	___	___	___	___	___	___
b. B.Com. (Hon.)	___	___	___	___	___	___
c. M.Com./MBA	___	___	___	___	___	___
d. M.Phil.	___	___	___	___	___	___
e. Ph.D.	___	___	___	___	___	___
f. Diploma/Certi-ficate	___	___	___	___	___	___

10. Courses of Study :

	Graduate Degree	Post-Graduate Degree	Certificate/ Diploma
a. Title of Degree awarded	______	______	______
b. Total Number of Courses offered	______	______	______
c. Number of Accounting Courses in (b) above	______	______	______
d. Teaching Hours provided for each Course (per week)	______	______	______
e. Teaching Hours provided for Accounting Courses (per week)	______	______	______

11. Subjects of Study Prescribed: (Please tick mark (×) at appropriate Place :

Subject	Graduate Degree	Post-graduate Degree	Certificate/ Diploma
a. Company Accounts	______	______	______
b. Advanced Accounting	______	______	______
c. Principles of Audit	______	______	______
d. Management Audit	______	______	______
e. Cost Audit	______	______	______
f. Taxation (Direct Taxes)	______	______	______
g. Taxation (Indirect Taxes)	______	______	______
h. Taxation (Sales Tax)	______	______	______
i. Taxation -Tax Planning & Mgt.	______	______	______
j. Elements of Cost Accounting	______	______	______
k. Advanced Cost Accounting	______	______	______
l. Management Accounting	______	______	______
m. Financial Management	______	______	______
n. Investment Mgt.	______	______	______
o. Business Statistics	______	______	______
p. Research Methodology	______	______	______

q. Operations Research & Q.T.	______	______	______
r. Accounting Theory	______	______	______
s. Computer Accounting	______	______	______

Note : Please send a copy of latest syllabus prescribed for Degree/Post-graduate/Certificate/Diploma examinations.

12. Is there a provision for practical/on the job training in Accounting courses?

Yes/No

13. If yes, for what period it is prescribed? ______________
What is the arrangement for training? ______________

Note : Please attach a separate note, if required.

14. Teaching :
(a) Method of Teaching adopted by the Department/Faculty (Case Method/Lecture Method)
(b) Medium of Instructions: English/Hindi/Regional Language

15. Examinations:

	Graduate Degree		Post-graduate Degree		Diploma/ Certificate
a. Nomenclature of Examination	——		——		——
b. Frequency of Examinations (Annual/Semester)	——		——		——
c. Performance at Examinations	——		——		——
(Last five years)	1995	1991	1990	1989	1988
i. Number of students appearing	—	—	—	—	—
ii. Number of students Qualifying	—	—	—	—	—

16. Research in Accounting:

a. Number of Qualified Supervisors in the Department of Commerce/Accounting ______

b. Total Number of Research Scholars Registered ______

c. Total Number of Scholars awarded Ph.D. degree last year ________

d. Major Areas and Topics of Research in Accounting :

 1. ________________________________
 2. ________________________________
 3. ________________________________
 4. ________________________________

e. Arrangement in the University for Registration of new scholars:

____

____

Note : Please enclose a copy of the regulations for Ph.D. degree.

f. What are the forums for research in Accounting? (Briefly describe the activities of these forums) __________

____

g. Research Publications of the Department of Commerce/ Accounting?

____

____

Note : Please give a list.

17. Liaison with other Institutions:

 a. Prescribed Courses of Study:

  i. Are Faculty members from University consulted by Committees prescribing syllabus for Courses?

  Yes/No

  ii. Are Professional Accountants consulted by the Committee prescribing syllabus for Institutes?

  Yes/No

 b. Teaching:

  i. Are Faculty members associated with Teaching of Courses by Institutes?

  Yes/No

  ii. Is any Professional Accountant associated with Teaching work in the University?

  Yes/No

c. Evaluation:

i. Are Faculty members associated with evaluation by the Institutes?

Yes/No

ii. Is any Professional Accountant associated with evaluation in the University?

Yes/No

d. Administration:

i. Are Faculty members associated with administration in the Institutes?

Yes/No

ii. Is any Professional Accountant associated with administration of the University/Department?

Yes/No

e. Continuing Education Programme:

Are Seminars, Conferences, Workshops and other continuing education programmes organized by the University in liaison with the Institutes?

Yes/No

f. Research Programmes:

Are Research projects undertaken by the University/ Department/Faculty Members jointly with the Institutes?

Yes/No

g. Credit in Examinations:

i. Is credit/exemption given to students qualifying at the examinations of the Institutes at the University examinations?

Yes/No

ii. Is credit/exemption given to students qualifying at University examinations at the examinations of the Institutes?

Yes/No

h. Membership:

i. Are members of faculty from Universities allowed enrolment as members of the Institutes?

Yes/No

ii. Are members of Institutes considered as qualified to teach in the University?

Yes/No

18. Educational Extension Programmes :
    i. Are educational extension programmes organized by the Department of Commerce/Accounting?

Yes/No

ii. If yes, give the following information:

	Number of Programmes Organized	Number of Persons Benefited
a. For Government	______	______
b. For Public Sector Enterprises	______	______
c. For Private Sector Companies	______	______
d. For Professional Accountants	______	______
e. Any other (specify)	______	______
Total		

19. Employment Opportunities:
    a. Identify the areas of employment for students with specialization in Accounting (Give percentages)

	Industry/ Trade/ Transport	Finan- cial Institu- tions	Govern- ment Depart- ments	Self Employ- ment
a. Graduates	____	____	____	____
b. Post-graduates	____	____	____	____
c. Diploma/Certificate Holders	____	____	____	____

b. What type of Jobs are generally taken up Clerical/ Supervisory/Managerial by Commerce/Accounting Graduates? Others (please specify)________________________

____

c. i. Is there a placement officer?

Yes/No

If yes, what is his role? (Please specify) __________

____

ii. Is there an alumni association/old boys association?

Yes/No

If yes, what is its role? (Please specify) ____________

____

20. What problems are generally experienced in conducting educational programmes of Commerce/Accounting?

a. While Designing Courses of Study ____________

____

b. While Conducting Teaching ______________

____

c. Examinations ______________

____

Note: Please give a brief note.

21. What are the future plans of the Department? Please specify.

____

____

____

____

22. Brief History of the Faculty/Department:

(Note: Please give years of starting different courses and special papers, details of Seminars, Conferences, other academic programmes organized, names of Heads of Department, Professors, etc.

____

____

____

____

23. General observations on the status of Accounting Education in the University/Region/Country.

____

____

____

____

Place (Signatures & Name of Respondent)

Date Organization/Institution

APPENDIX 1.B

ACCOUNTING EDUCATION IN THE COUNTRIES OF SOUTH ASIAN REGION

Questionnaire for Institutes of Professional Accountants

1. Name and Complete Address of the Institute : ____________
2. Year of Establishment : ____________
3. Names of President, Vice-President and Secretary of the Institute: ____________
4. Membership:
   a. Type of Membership offered Associate / Fellow / Both
   b. Qualification for Membership
      Educational ____________
      Others ____________
   c. Total Number of Members on roll during last five years : 1987 1991 1990 1989 1988
      _____ _____ _____ _____ _____

5. Enrolment of Trainees:
   a. Mode of Entry: ____________
   b. Educational Qualification for New Entrants ____________
   c. Period of Training ____________
   d. Method of Academic Instructions ____________
   e. Type of Training:
      Theoretical guidance/On the Job training/Full-time Involvement in day to day work (Please specify) ______
   f. Facilities Provided by the Institute to students:
      i. Books & Study Material
         Yes/No
      ii. Guidance Notes for Examinations
         Yes/No
      iii. Free Residential Accommodation
         Yes/No

iv. Free Meals

Yes/No

v. Transportation Facility

Yes/No

vi. Any other (Please specify) ____________

g. Facility provided by members to trainees enrolled ____________

7. Examinations :

a. Examination	Educational Qualification	Total Period	Number of courses offered	Frequency of Examination
Entrance/ Foundation	________	____	______	________
Intermediate	________	____	______	________
Final	________	____	______	________
Others :				
i.	________	____	______	________
ii.	________	____	______	________
iii.	________	____	______	________

b. Results of Examinations for last five years:

Year	Number of Candidates Appearing	Number Qualifying Candidates	Percentage
1995	——	———	———
1991	——	———	———
1990	——	———	———
1989	——	———	———
1988	——	———	———

8. Facilities provided by the Institute for Continuing Education to Members:
   a. Number of Seminars and Symposiums Organised _____
   b. Number of Orientation Programmes Organised _______
   c. Number of Extension Lectures/Discussion

Sessions Organized ______

d. Number of Other Programmes Organized ______

9. Liaison with Universities:

i. Are Faculty Members from Universities Consulted by Committees Prescribing Syllabus for Examinations?

Yes/No

ii. Association with Examinations

Yes/No

iii. Evaluation at Examinations

Yes/No

iv. Administration of Institute

Yes/No

v. Continuing Education Programmes/Seminars/Conferences/Workshops/Extension Lectures/Symposiums etc.

Yes/No

b. Are Faculty Members from Universities Enrolled as Members of the Institute?

Yes/No

10. Contribution to Research in Accounting:

a. i. Number of Research Projects Financed ______

ii. Total Financial Assistance Provided (Rs.) ______

b. i. Number of Research Publications ______

ii. Expenditure on Research Publications (Rs.) ______

11. Liaison with Other Institutes:

(Please specify the nature and form of inter-Institute cooperation) ______

______

______

______

12. Major Problems faced by the Institute in Enrolment, Training and Examinations:

______

______

______

______

13. Future Plans of the Institute:
    a. Regarding Enrolment of New Entrants: ____________
    b. Education and Training of New Entrants ____________
    c. Examination System ____________
    d. Continuing Education of Members ____________
    e. Liaison with Universities ____________
    f. Liaison with Other Institutes ____________

14. Areas of Employment/Professional Work for the Members:
    a. In Government ____________
    b. In Public Sector ____________
    c. In Private Sector ____________
    d. As Professional Accountants ____________
    e. Any other (Please specify) ____________

15. History of the Institute: (Please give a brief note)

____

Place (Name and Signatures of Respondent)
Date Organisation/Institute

APPENDIX 1.C

Dr. K. R. Sharma
Professor, Chairman of Faculty & Dean
College of Commerce &
Management Studies
M. L. Sukhadia University

Phone College 412 009
Residence 412 986
Residence :
C-1, Durga Nursery
Road
Udaipur - 313 001
(India)

No. CCMS /PA/93/
Dated 18th April, 1993

Dr/Professor................

Subject : Accounting Education in the Countries of South Asian Region.

Dear Sir,

Some time back vide letter No. CCMS/PA/92 dated 18-01-1992 I had floated a questionnaire for collecting certain information for the research project on the above subject. However, we have not received any response from your end. Since there has been a long time gap and the work of the project is held up for this reason I request you to please trace the papers, get the questionnaire filled and dispatch it at an early date. In case the questionnaire is not readily available please feel free to write us. A fresh copy of the questionnaire is being enclosed for your use.

Hoping to receive an early response and with thanks.

Yours sincerely,

(K.R. Sharma)

LIST OF RESPONDENTS

Institutes of Professional Accountants:

1. Institute of Chartered Accountants of India, New Delhi
2. Institute of Cost & Works Accountants of India, Calcutta
3. Institute of Chartered Accountants of Pakistan, Karachi
4. Institute of Cost & Management Accountants of Pakistan, Karachi
5. Institute of Chartered Accountants of Bangladesh, Dhaka
6. Institute of Cost & Management Accountants of Bangladesh, Dhaka
7. Institute of Chartered Accountants of Sri Lanka, Colombo

Foreign Universities:

Bangladesh

1. Dhaka University, Dhaka
2. Rajshahi University, Rajshahi
3. Chittgong University, Chittgong

Bhutan:

1. Sherubtse College at Kanglung, Bhutan

India:

01. Mohan Lal Sukhadia University, Udaipur - Rajasthan
02. University of Rajasthan, Jaipur - Rajasthan
03. Jai Narayan Vyas University, Jodhpur - Rajasthan
04. Maharshi Dayanand Saraswati Univeristy, Ajmer - Rajasthan
05. Gujarat University, Ahmedabad - Gujarat
06. Saurastra University, Rajkot - Gujarat
07. M.S.University of Baroda, Baroda - Gujarat
08. Jiyaji University, Gwalior - Madhya Pradesh
09. Doctor Hari Singh Gour Vishwavidalaya, Sagar - Madhya Pradesh
10. Vikram University, Ujjain - Madhya Pradesh
11. Delhi University, Delhi
12. Punjab University, Chandigarh - Punjab

13. Punjabi University, Patiala - Punjab
14. Kurukshetra University, Kurukshetra - Haryana
15. Maharshi Dayanand University, Rohtak - Haryana
16. Banaras Hindu University, Varanasi - Uttar Pradesh
17. Mahatma Gandhi Kashi Vidyapeeth, Varanasi - Uttar Pradesh
18. Lucknow University, Lucknow - Uttar Pradesh
19. Calcutta University, Calcutta - West Bengal
20. Gauhati University, Guwahati - Assam
21. Manipur University, Imphal - Manipur
22. Utkal University, Bhuwaneshwar - Orrisa
23. Goa University, Goa
24. Mysore University, Mysore - Karnataka
25. Bangalore University, Bangalore - Karnataka
26. Andhra University, Visakhapatnam - Andhra Pradesh

Nepal

1. Tribhuwan University, Kirtipur Kathmandu

Pakistan

1. University of Punjab, Lahore
2. Gomal University, Dera Ismail Khan (NWFP)
3. Quaid-i-Azam University, Islamabad
4. Karachi University, Karachi
5. Azad Jammu Kashmir University, Kotli, Azad Kashmir

Sri Lanka

1. University of Colombo, Colombo
2. University of Jaffna, Jaffna
3. University of Kelaniya,Vidyalankara
4. University of Ruhuwa, Ruhuwa
5. University of Peradeniya, Peradenai
6. University of Jayawardenepura, Vidyodaya

APPENDIX 1.E

EMBASSIES AND HIGH COMMISSIONS OF THE SAARC COUNTRIES IN INDIA

1. High Commission of Bangladesh
   56-M, Ring Road
   Lajpat Nagar III
   New Delhi - 110 024

2. Embassy of Bhutan
   Chandragupta Marg
   Chanakyapuri
   New Delhi - 110 021

3. Embassy of Nepal
   Barakhamba Road
   New Delhi - 110 001

4. High Commission of Pakistan
   2/50 G, Shanti Path
   Chanakyapuri
   New Delhi - 110 021

5. High Commission of Sri Lanka
   27, Kautilya Marg
   Chanakyapuri
   New Delhi - 110 021

APPENDIX 4.A

UGC, CURRICULUM DEVELOPMENT CENTRE IN COMMERCE, 1989 – SUGGESTED COURSES AND SUBJECTS

B.Com. (Honors)

I year :

H.1.1 Business Organisation and Management
H.1.2 Business Laws
H.1.3 Business Economics
H.1.4 Environmental Studies
H.1.5 Financial Accounting
H.1.6 Business Mathematics and Computer Awareness
H.1.7 Communication Skill

II Year :

H.2.1 Higher Financial Accounting
H.2.2 Cost Accounting
H.2.3 Production Management
H.2.4 Financial Management
H.2.5 Monetary Economics
H.2.6 Statistics

III Year :

H.3.1 Income Tax Law
H.3.2 Auditing
H.3.3 Personnel Management
H.3.4 Marketing Management
H.3.5 International Trade
H.3.6 Public Finance

B.Com (Professional)

I Year :

P.1.1 Business Organisation
P.1.2 Business Laws
P.1.3 Business Economics
P.1.4 Environmental Studies

P.1.5 Financial Accounting
P.1.6 Business Mathematics and Computer Awareness
P.1.7 Communication Skill

II Year :
P.2.1 Cost Accounting
P.2.2 Accounting Practices for Small Units
P.2.3 Financial Management
P.2.4 Factory Organisation and Management
P.2.5 Statistics
P.2.6 Indian Financial System

III Year :

I Accounting :
P.3.A.1 Company Accounting
P.3.A.2 Computer Concepts and Cobol Programming
P.3.A.3 Auditing
P.3.A.4 Taxation (Customs & Central Excise)
P.3.A.5 Taxation (Income Tax)
P.3.A.6 Taxation (Wealth, Gift, Sales Tax and State Excise)

II Business Studies :
P.3.BS. 1 Personnel Management
P.3.BS. 2 Labour Laws
P.3.BS. 3 Industrial Relations
P.3.BS. 4 Marketing Practices
P.3.BS. 5 Advertising Management
P.3.BS. 6 Sales Management

III Business Economics :
P.3.BE. 1Foreign Trade and its Financing
P.3.BE. 2 Import Policy and Procedures
P.3.BE. 3 Export Policy and Procedures
P.3.BE. 4 Commercial Banking Operations
P.3.BE. 5 Banking Law and Practice
P.3.BE. 6 Cooperative Banking

M.Com. (Accounting)

A.01 Higher Company Accounts
A.02 Accounting Theory
A.03 Management Accounting
A.04 Management Control System
A.05 International Accounting
A.06 Operations Research and Computer Applications
A.07 Financial Management
A.08 Theory and Practice of Statistics
A.09 Direct Tax Laws
A.10 Tax Planning and Management
A.11 Investment Management

M.Com. (Business Studies)

BS.01 Principles of Management
BS.02 Organisational Behaviour and Industrial Psychology
BS.03 Financial Management
BS.04 Marketing Management
BS.05 Personnel Management
BS.06 Production and Operations Management
BS.07 Business Policy and Environment
BS.08 Accounting for Business Decisions
BS.09 Management Information System
BS.10 Public Enterprise Management
BS.11 Security Analysis and Portfolio Management
BS.12 Theory and Practice of Statistics

M.Com. (Business Economics)

BE.01 Micro Economics
BE.02 Macro Economics
BE.03 Industrial Economics
BE.04 Theory and Practice of Statistics
BE.05 Economic Growth and Planning
BE.06 Financial Markets and Institutions
BE.07 International Economic Relations
BE.08 Industrial Relations and Personnel Management

BE.09 Public Enterprise Management
BE.10 Public Budgeting
BE.11 Monetary Policy

P.G. Diploma in Accountancy and Internal Audit

1.01 Management Accounting
1.02 Financial Management
1.03 Financial Accounting and Auditing
1.04 Internal Audit

P.G. Diploma in Insurance

2.01 Principles of Life Insurance
2.02 Fire and Marine Insurance
2.03 Property and Liability Insurance
2.04 Insurance Finance Administration

P.G. Diploma in Cost Accounting

3.01 Production Management
3.02 Cost Records and Overheads
3.03 Costing Methods and Techniques
3.04 Cost and Management Audit

P.G. Diploma in Personnel Management

4.01 Foundation of Personnel Management
4.02 Industrial Relations
4.03 Labour Legislation
4.04 Human Resource Development

P.G. Diploma in Portfolio Management

5.01 Security Analysis and Investment Decisions
5.02 Indian Capital Market
5.03 Financial Reporting and Analysis
5.04 Legal Framework

P.G. Diploma in Entrepreneurship and Small Unit Management

6.01 Entrepreneurship and Industrial Development
6.02 Project Planning and Management
6.03 Management of Small Enterprises
6.04 Finance and Tax Management

P.G. Diploma in Public Enterprises

7.01 Growth and Management of Public Enterprises
7.02 Human Resource Management
7.03 Financial Management
7.04 Public Accountability and Relations

P.G. Diploma in Foreign Trade

8.01 International Marketing and Management
8.02 Export Import Procedures and Documentation
8.03 Economic Systems and Foreign Trade in India
8.04 Commercial Laws and Overseas Marketing Research

APPENDIX 4.B

MOHAN LAL SUKHADIA UNIVERSITY, UDAIPUR, INDIA – FACULTY OF COMMERCE –

B.Com

I Year

1. Financial Accounting
2. Business Statistics
3. Management
4. Business Laws
5. Economic Environment in India
6. Business Economics

II Year

1. Income Tax Law and Accounts
2. Cost Accounting
3. Company Law and Secretarial Practice
4. Functional Management
5. Financial Management
6. Banking Law and Practice in India

III Year

1. Management Accounting
2. Auditing, or
   Taxation - Wealth Tax Gift Tax
   Central and Rajasthan Sales Tax, or
   Application of Computer in Accounting, or
   Quantitative Techniques & Operations Research
3. Stock Exchange and Securities
4. Human Resource Development, or
   Sales Management, or
   Business Environment, or
   Industrial Laws
5. International Trade and Finance
6. Money Banking & Public Finance

M.Com. - Accountancy & Statistics

Previous

1. Higher Accounting
2. Advanced Cost Accounting
3. Research Methodology & Quantitative Techniques
4. Tax Laws and Tax Planning

Final

1. Accounting Theory
2. Accounting Information System, or
   Security Analysis & Portfolio Management
3. International Financial Management
4. Contemporary Auditing
5. Accounting Application in Functional Management, or
   Project Planning, Appraisal and Control, or
   Managerial Economics, or
   Dissertation

M. Phil. - Accountancy & Statistics

1. Accounting Research Methods
2. Accounting Theory
3. Contemporary Issues in Accounting
4. Dissertation

BIBLIOGRAPHY

Books

Accountability in Higher Education, Association of Indian Universities, New Delhi, 1995

Adams, Don and Robert, M. Bjork, *Education in Developing Areas,* David Mckay Co., New York 1969

Agrawal, Govind Ram, *Higher Education for Business in Developing Nations like Nepal,* Center for Economic Development and Administration, Kathmandu, Nepal, 1974

Ahluwalia, S.P. and Bais, H.S., *Education Issues and Challenges*, Ashish Publishing House, Delhi

Amarchand, D. (Ed.) *Research Methods in Commerce*, Emrald Publications, 1987

Ansari, M. M., *Cost Effectiveness in Higher Education*, Concept Publishing Company, New Delhi, 1997

Ansari, M.M., *Education and Economic Development,* Association of Indian Universities, New Delhi, 1987

Banerjee, B., *Accounting Education in India,* DSA in Commerce, University of Calcutta, Calcutta, 1994

Bhandari, S.K.R., *A Survey of Research in Accounting Theory,* Indian Council of Social Sciences Research, New Delhi, 1976

Bhaurali, D., *Commerce Education in India,* Deep and Deep Publications, New Delhi, 1987

Daoyang, Guo, *The Past, Present and Future of Accounting Education of China,* Zhongnan University of Finance and Economics, Wuhan, The People's Republic of China, 1987

Dasgupta, L.R., *Business Education – A Dossier,* Research Board, City College, Commerce Department, 1959

Enthoven, Adolf J.H., *Accounting Education in Economic Development Management*, North Holland Publishing Company,1981

Hendriksen, *Accounting Theory*, Richard D. Irwin, Inc., New York, 1982

Kapadia, G.P., *History of Accounting Profession in India, Vol. I,* The Institute of Chartered Accountants of India, New Delhi, 1972

Khanzode, V.V., *Recent Trends in Commerce and Management Education,* Sterling Publishers Private Limited, New Delhi, 1990

Littleton, A.C., *Accounting Evolution to 1990*, American Institute Publishing Co., Inc. New York

Porwal, L.S., *Accounting Theory - An Introduction*, Tata McGraw Hill, New Delhi, 1993

Romharre and Roger Lamb, *The Encyclopaedic Dictionary of Psychology*, Basil Blackwell Publishers Ltd., Oxford England, 1983

Roy, G.D., *A Survey of Accounting Ideas*, Alpha Publishing Concern, Calcutta, 1963

SAARC Chamber of Commerce & Industry, *Study on Opportunities for Intra-Regional Investment Cooperation Among SAARC Countries*, Abhinav Publishing Industries Pvt. Ltd., Delhi, 1997

Saeed, M., *A Survey of Research in Commerce and Management*, Anmol Publications, New Delhi, 1991

Shah, S.Y. (Ed.), *New Technologies in Higher Education*, Association of Indian Universities, New Delhi, 1986

Singh, Nirmal, *Education Under Seize*, Concept Publishing House, New Delhi, 1983

Society, *Education and Development*, Association of Indian Universities, New Delhi, 1998

South Asian Federation of Accountants Handbook, The Institute of Chartered Accountants of India, New Delhi, 1999

Uberoi, N.K. (Ed.), *Professional Competency in Higher Education*, Centre for Professional Development in Higher Education, University of Delhi, Delhi, 1995

UGC Occasional Paper No. 1, *Performance and Accountability in Higher Education*, University Grants Commission, New Delhi, 1994

UGC Occasional Paper No.2, *On Pricing Higher Education*, (Jandhyala B.G. Tilak), University Grants Commission, New Delhi, 1995

Zakir Hussain, *Education and National Development*, (Translated by Prof. Sheik Ali) Har Anand Publication, New Delhi

Zeff, Stephen A., and Thomas F. Keller, *Financial Accounting Theory I - Issues and Controversies*, McGraw Hill Book Company, New York, 1973

Reports

Accounting Education Change Commission, Position Statement No. One - *Objectives of Education For Accountants*, American Accounting Association, September 1990

Accounting Education Change Commission, Position Statement No. Two - *The First Course in Accounting*, American Accounting Association, June 1992

Accounting Education Change Commission, Issues Statement No. 1 - *AECC Urges Priority For Teaching in Higher Education*, American Accounting Association, August 1990

Accounting Education Change Commission, Issues Statement No. 2 - *AECC Urges De-coupling of Academic Studies and Professional Accounting Examination Preparation,* American Accounting Association, July 1991

Accounting Education Change Commission, Issues Statement No. 3 - *The Importance of Two Year Colleges for Accounting Education*, American Accounting Association, August 1992

Accounting Education Change Commission, Issues Statement No. 4 - *Improving the Early Employment Experience of Accountants*, American Accounting Association, April 1993

Accounting Education Change Commission, Issues Statement No. 5 - *Evaluating and Rewarding Effective Teaching*, American Accounting Association, April 1993

Commonwealth Universities Yearbook, The Association of Commonwealth Universities, 1988

Curriculum Development Center Report, University Grants Commission, New Delhi, 1989

Handbook on Management Education, Association of Indian Universities, New Delhi, 1997

IFAC Exposure Draft, *The Chartered Accountant*, July 1986

National Policy on Education, 1968, Resolution Passed by the Parliament of India, 1968

National Policy on Education, 1986, A Resolution Passed by the Parliament of India, 1986

Report of Secondary Education Commission, 1952-53 (Dr. A. Laxmanswami Mudaliar Commission), Ministry of Education, Government of India, New Delhi, 1953

Report of the Committee on Alternative Models of Management (Gnanam Committee), University Grants Commission, New Delhi

Report of the Committee on Standards of University Education, 1961 (Prof. N.K. Sidhanta Committee) University Grants Commission, New Delhi, 1965

Report of the Curriculum Development Center in Commerce, University Grants Commission, New Delhi, 1989

Report of the Education Commission: Education and National Development, 1964-66 (Commission under the Chairmanship of Prof. D.S. Kothari), Ministry of Education, Government of India, New Delhi, 1966

Report of the National Commission on Teachers-II 1983-85, Ministry of Education, Government of India, The Controller of Publications, Delhi

Report of the Review Committee, National Policy on Education 1986, Committee appointed by the Central Advisory Board on Education, January 1992

Report of the Review Committee for Accounting Education, The Institute of Chartered Accountants of India, New Delhi, June 1979

Report of the Review Committee on Education, 1960 (Prof. N.K. Sidhanta Committee) University Grants Commission, New Delhi, 1960

Report of the Special Committee on Education and Training of Chartered Accountants, The Institute of Chartered Accountants of Pakistan, August 1988

Report of the University Education Commission December 1948 - August 1949 (Radha Krishanan Committee) Manager Publications, Government of India, Simla, 1950

Seventy-third Report of Public Accounts Committee, 1977-78 of the Sixth Lok Sabha, Lok Sabha Secretariat, New Delhi

UGC Funding of Institutions of Higher Education (Report of Justice K. Punnaya Committee 1992-93), University Grants Commission, New Delhi

Universities and Research, Association of Indian Universities, New Delhi, 1980

Universities Handbook, Association of Indian Universities, New Delhi, 1997

Articles

Anand Sarup, "*University Autonomy and Accountability*", UGC Occasional Paper No 1, University Grants Commission, New Delhi, May 1994

Bhagwati Prasad, "Presidential Speech at the XXI Annual Conference of Indian Accounting Association at Bangalore", January-February 1998, *Indian Journal of Accounting,* June, 1998

Bhandari, S.K.R., "*Education for Accounting in India - A Perspective for Development*", Presidential Address at the Third Annual Conference of IAA, February 1973

Daoyang, Guo, "*The Past, Present and Future of Accounting Education of China*", Zhongnan University of Finance and Economics, Wuhan, The People's Republic of China, 1987

Dutta, Manipadma, Accounting Education and Research in India: An Overview, *Indian Journal of Accounting,* Vol. XXII, December, 1991

Garg, Subhash, Restructuring Public Expenditure on Education, *Management Perspective,* Vol. I No. 1, July, 1998

Grover, R.K., Accounting Education: Need for Professional Approach by University, *The Indian Journal of Commerce*, Vol. 51 No. 1, March 1988

Gupta, Sanjeev, Benedict Clement and Erwin Tiongson, 'Public Spending on Human Development', *Finance &*

Development, International Monetary Fund, New York, September 1998

Kawakita, Hiroshi, "*Current Status and Development of Accounting Education in CAPA*", (Mimiographed, 1987)

Khandelwal, N.M., Accounting Education in India - Current Issues, *Indian Journal of Accounting*, Vol. XXIII, June 1992

Needles, Belverd E. Jr., Global Guidelines for Accounting Education: Regulation, Reciprocity and Implementation, *Indian Accounting Association Research Foundation*, January 1999

Phillip, G. Altbach, "Pattern in Higher Education Development Towards the Year 2000", *Journal of Higher Education*, Vol. 15, 1989-90

Sharma, K.R., Present Status and Problems of Accounting Education in Nepal, *Indian Journal of Accounting*, Vol., XVII, December 1987

____ ____, Accounting Education - Some Areas of Wider Concern, Paper presented at the XVI Annual Conference of Indian Accounting Association at Jodhpur December 23-25, 1991

____ ____, Presidential Address at the XX Annual Conference of Indian Accounting Association at Goa, February 1997, *Indian Journal of Accounting*, June 1997

____ ____, International Accounting - Some Important Issues, paper presented at the Seminar on Internationalisation of Accounting: Challenges and Opportunities under the joint auspices of ICAI and MLSU at Udaipur on 10th August 1997

____ ____, Total Quality People: Transforming Challenges into Opportunities Through Education, Keynote Speech at the XXIX National Convension of Indian Society for Training and Development on People Technology Interface, November 5-7, 1998

____ ____, Accounting in the Next Millennium, Keynote Speech at the National Seminar on Public Interest Accounting, April, 1999, *Accounting Review*, December 1999

Sishtla, Vijaya Saradhi, Economic Planning and Accounting Education in University, *Indian Journal of Accounting*, Vol. XIX, June 1989

Sundararajan, S., Structure and Performance of University Commerce Education - Relevance of Professional Courses, paper presented at the All India Conference on Accounting Standards and Practical Orientation to Commerce Education, Mysore University, Mysore, August 9 -10, 1990

Takwale, R.G., Higher Education Changes and Reforms, Society, *Education and Development,* Association of Indian Universities, New Delhi, 1998

Vinaya Swaroop, "Education and Health Care in the Caribbean", *Finance and Development,* International Monetary Fund, June 1997

Williams, Doyle Z., Reforming Accounting Education, *Journal of Accountancy*, August 1993

INDEX